YOU DID
WHAT?

YOU DID WHAT?

Secrets, Confessions & Outrageous Stories from Real Life

TOVA LEIGH

WATKINS
Sharing Wisdom Since 1893

This edition first published in the UK and USA in 2021
by Watkins, an imprint of Watkins Media Limited
Unit 11, Shepperton House
89–93 Shepperton Road
London
N1 3DF

enquiries@watkinspublishing.com

Design and typography copyright © Watkins Media Limited 2021

Text copyright © Tova Leigh 2021

Tova Leigh asserts her right under the Copyright, Designs
and Patents Act 1988 to be identified as the author of this work.

10 9 8 7 6 5 4 3 2 1

Designed and typeset by Watkins

Printed and bound in the UK by TJ Books Ltd

A CIP record for this book is available from the British Library

ISBN: 978-1-78678-550-3 (Hardback)
        978-1-78678-575-6 (e-book)

www.watkinspublishing.com

Contents

Contents

Introduction

Everyone loves secrets. Not having them, of course – especially if they are big secrets. Carrying those can be draining. But hearing them – now, that's a different story. Everyone loves hearing secrets, other people's secrets.

There is something exciting about the fact no one else knows something, and most of us are also a little nosy, even if we don't like admitting it. I don't know how the experts would explain why hearing other people's secrets is so appealing, all I know is this: everyone likes a good secret, everyone has secrets and, finally, most of us feel better when we share our secrets with others.

Now that's not a given, especially if you're hiding something big from someone close to you. But over the past five years I have heard everything, from cheating and revenge stories to confessions of never spoken loves and abusive relationships, "mom" secrets, wife secrets, secrets from the bedroom and the boardroom, holiday secrets, sexual fantasies, online dating, and so many poop confessions . . . You wouldn't believe how many people out there have shat themselves.

I figure some of you might like to know WHY I wanted to write a confessions book to begin with, or maybe you're hoping to hear some of my own secrets. To be honest, I've already written about some of the most intimate parts of my life in my previous book, *F*cked at 40*. I have a feeling nothing I have left to say would shock you . . . apart from the fact I sit in the shower.

I honestly thought this was normal until that day, a few years ago, when my husband, Mike, walked in on me and found me sitting down on the shower floor, singing "Rainbow High" from the *Evita* soundtrack at the top of my voice. He looked at me in a way he had never done before and said, "Are you okay? Did you fall down?" He says this is a strange thing to do and I didn't even realize it. But after I "came out" as a shower-sitter I found out that many people sit in the shower. Some people even have a little stool, which frankly I think is genius, but I fear Mike will never allow it. The point is that what could have been a real cause of shame (yes, I'm being slightly sarcastic) became something we laugh about because I'm not the only one who does it.

And that's the key – not being the only one.

I discovered that many things I did, and thought I was the only one, were actually more common than they seemed, and the way I discovered this was through hearing others' confessions.

Five years ago I started a Facebook page called "My Thoughts About Stuff". It was a place for me to vent my frustrations and struggles as a new mom. The whole premise of the page was to come out and say the things no one admits out loud, like how hard being a parent is. And not just because of the sleepless nights and how expensive children are, but also because kids can be selfish assholes who ruin your sex life and pelvic floor muscles, plus you never get to go anywhere nice any more or even to the toilet without an audience. In short – all the things that are never mentioned in parenting books.

My point is, the Facebook page was all about sharing my deepest secrets, the things I feared people would judge me for if only they knew. It was a place for me to say my truth, and soon it became a place for many other parents, especially moms, to say their truths too.

I realized very quickly that there was something freeing about being honest, especially when it was met with the words "I do that too" or "I feel the same way". I guess there was something comforting about knowing no one was perfect, we were all in the same boat, and everyone was just as miserable as each other. But in a nice way.

And that's how the idea for my live online show, Pyjama Party & Confessions, came about – which is what this book is based on. The children were still young and so going out on a Friday night simply wasn't something I did, and I thought to myself there must be so many parents who, like me, have young kids and can't go out but would love to do something fun on a Friday night, so why not do it together?

So I decided that every Friday night we would have a party on Facebook. The format was very simple: I would go live from my bedroom, in my pyjamas, on my bed, broadcasting to people all over the world. We would all have a drink (I had a few) and I would read out confessions people had sent in advance, then we would vote and each week there would be a winner, and we would all have a laugh. It was a way to connect with the online community I had built and a means to connect parents with each other.

I clearly remember the first ever Pyjama Party and how nervous I was. I had no idea if anyone would show up, if anyone would send in a confession or if people would even like it. I made my bed. This was not something I normally did. Don't judge me but I'm from the "what's the point in tidying it up if it's only going to get messed up again in a few hours" camp. Yet on that Friday (and many other Fridays after that) not only did I make my bed, I even threw some doughnut pillows someone had sent me for the girls onto the bed to make it look a little more "party-like". People fell in love with them and they became part of the Pyjama Party & Confessions "set".

I debated what to wear. Do I go for pyjamas or a party outfit?! After all, it was meant to be an alternative to a night out so one could argue I could have dressed up, done my make-up and even brushed my hair. But then again it was also a PYJAMA party and my guess was that most people just wanted to relax and watch someone who looked as tired as they were. So I opted for Mike's pyjamas and a messy "mom bun" because comfy wins every time. Especially if you're a mom. Side note: in real life I don't actually wear pyjamas to bed, I'm more of a T-shirt with knickers kind of gal, but it's not as cute as it sounds, I'm talking big granny pants and a dingy T-shirt I should have chucked out ages ago. In fact, my favourite T-shirt to sleep in is this pink one I bought from Primark a few years ago for a cancer charity 5km-run which says "I have nothing to wear". And that pretty much sums it up.

I wasn't sure what time to start the party. I knew most parents like us would have to go through the dreaded bedtime routine before they could finally pop open a bottle of wine, but I also didn't want to start too late because most parents with young kids crash around 10pm.

At 8:30pm, UK time, I hit the "go live" button not knowing if anyone would tune in. A few people had sent in confessions in advance via my Facebook DMs. I remember one confession was from a mother who admitted that sometimes she hides from her kids in the pantry when she just can't take it any more. She wrote about feeling "mom guilt" for doing that and for having those moments, and that she never tells her husband how she feels. I could relate with that more than you can imagine. As a mother of three girls all born in the space of two years (we have twins), hiding was my middle name: pantry, toilet, garden ... You name it, I tried it. (The best hiding place, by the way, is the car because you can drive off.)

Another confession was about eating snacks when the kids aren't looking and not sharing. That mom admitted she tells her kids she is eating something spicy while really snacking on sweets and chocolates – which I am pretty sure she also stole from their Halloween stash. Again, this is something I have done so many times (and still do). I also used to tell my kids I was eating a pepper when in fact I was eating crisps to explain the crunchy sounds coming from my mouth. No idea how they fell for it for as long as they did, as they never physically saw me eating a pepper. Ever.

I think we had something like five confessions in total and most of them were about parenting and all kinds of little things. There was nothing groundbreaking about any of them but what was interesting was that, even though most of them were no big deal, and I personally was able to relate to all of them, the people who sent them in were harvesting immense amounts of guilt and shame for doing the things they were confessing about. I gave people the option to stay anonymous and most of them did, but they gave themselves nicknames like "playdough-hating mom" or "nappy change gone bad", which I thought was really funny. I remember asking people to share the live video when we started so that it would go on more timelines, something I still do to this day, and then adding "You might want to delete it later so your friends don't see what you get up to on a Friday night". It always amazes me how many people are happy to share these parties, now even more than back then, given how "dirty" the confessions are these days, but we'll get to that.

Anyway, I read the confessions out one by one, probably a little too fast because I didn't know if anyone would be at all interested but when I looked up, to my surprise, everyone absolutely loved them. The comment section lit up with everyone (virtually) screaming "OMG I DO THAT TOO!" And I knew we were onto something.

Pyjama Party & Confessions became a weekly thing after that, with people tuning in from around the globe, some watching in their early hours of the morning from Australia or their Friday afternoon from the US. You'd think that such a global community that included the Far East, America, Europe, the Middle East, South Africa and more would bring confessions that were very different and that every culture would have its own little quirks. But that's not what happened at all. We discovered TOGETHER that we are all far more similar than we think, and that humans have the same secrets no matter where they are from in the world, the colour of their skin or the language they speak.

I would read mom confessions from France, Germany, Turkey, Iran, the UK and America and they could have been from anywhere. One mom admitted she told her son that when the ice cream van played music it meant they'd run out of ice cream. So many women in the comment section said they had done something similar, and those who hadn't said it was a great mom hack and that they would start doing it from now on. It didn't matter the origin of the confession – parenting is hard for everyone, and the secrets people keep surrounding parenting are the same – not bonding with babies, not wanting children, loving them but also hating them, hiding from them, hiding stuff from them (especially snacks), feeling guilt, pretending to be unwell to get a "day off" ... Moms on all continents do it all.

Most importantly, as more and more people started sending in confessions each week, what became apparent is that everyone felt better after sharing their secrets and receiving feedback from everyone watching, which was always supportive and accepting.

And this was key.

Like the movie *Fight Club* with its one-rule policy, Pyjama Party also had only one rule, and that was – no judgement. People knew (and I reminded them every week) that no matter what I read out, we do not judge. It became a "safe space", which is very rare on social media and I think we all appreciated that.

That, plus the fact that many of the confessions were hilarious.

I don't care how many times I read a confession about someone shitting themselves, it gets me every time. We've had people confess to pooping in gardens, bins, bags and hats. We even had someone admit they pooped out of a window. She was staying the night at a boy's house – the first night over and still early in their relationship. You know, that stage when you still pretend that you are a superhuman who never farts or needs to go to the toilet. But after a heavy night of drinking and eating spicy foods, she needed a number two badly the following morning. From memory the guy had some issue with his toilet and she didn't want to risk the chance of it not going down when she flushed, so instead she stuck her butt out of the toilet window and just let it flow. If you think that's bad you can be sure we've had worse. Like out the window from a driving car worse!

Mike and I would often joke about this specific topic. There are so many confessions about it and I remember saying I didn't understand how anyone could reach that point where they needed to go so badly that pooping in the street would be a reasonable thing to do. Until a few months ago. I am not proud of this, and if it hadn't been for the past five years of doing Pyjama Party & Confessions, and reading so many poop-related confessions, I probably would have never admitted this. Yet one particular afternoon, I took off for my daily walk in the suburbs, and after ten minutes of walking found myself desperately needing to go to the point I could not take one more step and had to cross my legs and hope for the best. Luckily I had my phone on me so I rang Mike who was home with the girls and said, "Please come and get me, I am about to soil myself!" There was silence, and then a moment later he said, "What has happened to you?" I stood there, legs crossed, tears in my eyes waiting for him to arrive, praying I wouldn't run into anyone I knew for what felt an eternity. And in all that time I kept looking around me thinking, "Would it really be so bad if I stuck my bum into a street bin and just go for it?" You have to have been in that situation to fully understand the desperation, and I can tell you having been in that situation I will never question anyone else. Mike arrived a few minutes later, I fell into the car as he said, "This is your lowest moment." To which I could only moan, "I know."

It's funny how confessions have progressed over the years ...

When we started, most of the confessions were parenting related, with the majority coming from mothers. The main theme was "mom guilt" – having it, not having it, not living up to expectations, lying about feeling ill in order to get out of housework, hiding in various places, wanting to run away and so on. There were also confessions about living a lie. One lady confessed she never really loved her husband; someone else said they were bisexual in a straight marriage. Others confessed to being in love with their partner's best friend, sibling and even parents! But no matter what I read out, those listening did not judge, and more people than you'd expect admitted they could relate to each situation.

Gradually the confessions moved toward sex. I have no idea how, when or why it happened but these days the majority of the stories are about sex, with one of the most popular topics being vibrators and self-pleasure. We also moved from confessions – the things no one knows – to outrageous and very funny stories.

My all-time favourite story has got to be a confession sent in from a woman who bought a vibrator without telling her husband about it because she felt too embarrassed. It was one of those vibrators that doesn't actually look like a sex toy, if anything it looked like one of those facial exfoliator things you see ads for on social media, so when he came across it and asked what it was, she said it was for her face and that it reduced wrinkles. The confession was that he's been using it on his face ever since and she has still, to this day, not told him the truth. I love that story.

When it comes to vibrators, so many people confessed they hide their sex toys from their partners; some women said they didn't buy sex toys because they don't want their partners to be offended. Many women have confessed to never having an orgasm. For me, this is not surprising, even though I know it's something many women find hard to admit. The reason being that female pleasure as a subject is simply not discussed openly enough, even in 2021. A lot of people would rather not know. Or they are happy having a conversation from a male point of view, with women's pleasure being the last thing on their mind. Some people may think confessions about women's orgasms (or lack of) are not sensational enough and even boring, but I think they are so important.

There have obviously been many confessions about getting caught in the act, or catching parents red handed. This also seemed like something unlikely and baffled Mike and I until that night we were getting it on in bed after a few glasses of wine. I had my eyes shut and was imagining we were on a hot beach, and as Mike spooned me from behind I heard a little voice say, "Mommy." My nine-year-old was standing three steps away from the bed. To say I was mortified doesn't come close to describing how I felt.

I was in such a state of shock that I didn't even cover up or shout or hide, I just calmly answered, "Yes?" To which she replied, "So is this sex?"

I am aware that years of therapy will be needed. But that's not even the worst part of the story. After she went back to bed, Mike and I had a short debate about whether we should continue or not. (I'm not going to lie, it was a real mood killer.) We decided to carry on very quietly, convinced that she had gone back to sleep and couldn't hear us. This certainty was crushed after the big finale when we heard her little voice from the bottom of the stairs say, "Good night Mommy."

We laugh about it now and, as you will soon find out, many have similar stories – some more eye-watering than others. I think one of the best we've had over the years was from a woman who was having sex with her partner doggy-style when she suddenly felt a little tap on her butt. She thought that it was too gentle for her partner's usual touch, and then she discovered it was in fact her toddler who had climbed into bed with them.

Sex stories always get a great reaction. I think it's because the topic is still a little hard to talk about, but when people share their funny or embarrassing moments it sort of takes the edge off. The other topic people seem to have lots of confessions about are revenge stories, many of them about work colleagues. Or exes. Let's just say – never use a toothbrush you have at someone's house who you've just broken up with or done something shitty to. The amount of people who have used toothbrushes to clean their toilet as revenge will shock you.

When I went on tour last year, I decided to add confessions to my one-woman show. The second half was dedicated to stories sent in from those who attended the shows and, just like the online version, people voted for their favourite confession and the winner received a prize. The confessions were submitted anonymously, but nearly every time the person who won the best confession would stand up and own it. People would cheer and clap because it didn't really matter what the confession was about, what mattered was that they put themselves out there.

Sadly, we haven't had many confessions from men over the years, and the majority of my followers are women. Men seem to love listening and attending the parties though, and one of my all-time favourite confessions is from a guy – and actually from someone I know – my father-in-law. All it said was: "My son was conceived on an Air France flight to Paris."

I am sure some of you are wondering if there are any confessions I didn't read out. The answer is yes. I would never read out anything that involves people inflicting violence on others, but I am happy to say nothing sent in was ever of that nature. I try not to share things relating to people other than the confessor, especially if their identity could be revealed. And I do share traumatic confessions sometimes, because I can assure you not everything that is sent in is happy or funny. Some confessions are truly heart-breaking – like people confessing to not having love in their lives or having to hide their sexual preference, or when someone tells their story of sexual abuse that they have never told anyone about previously. The community would get behind those confessions even more fiercely and these would almost always "win" because it was the listeners' way to show their support.

And I guess that was the reason I decided to write this book.

This is a collection of confessions sent in by the same amazing community who, together with me, created the Pyjama Party & Confessions format on Facebook. They are everyday people like me and you from all around the world, telling their stories and secrets in their own voices, and reminding us that we are all more alike than we care to admit.

Parenting Confessions

Last week I was so fed up with my kids and their smart ass behaviour that I decided to (for once) follow through on one of my regular warnings: "Your behaviour will have consequences." (It never does.) After a few days of having had enough, I had reached the absolute top of how much cheek and bullshit I was capable of taking, as a parent and a human being. So when they did not listen to me for the one-millionth time, I snapped. Into the kitchen I marched, took the cupcakes they had lovingly placed in the fridge earlier that day and were looking forward to eating later, and threw them in the bin. Then I proceeded to take a wooden spoon and stab the cupcakes in the bin repeatedly, screaming, "No one is getting the cupcakes!" the whole time. When I eventually came to,

I realized that no one could hear me because my husband was blowing away the leaves on our driveway and the noise from the leafblower drowned out my deranged yelling and stabbing of cupcakes.

I don't know what's more of a confession here – the fact I did that, the fact I didn't feel guilty afterwards, or the fact I didn't tell my husband about any of it.

He walked in after he had finished with the leaves and asked, "Everything okay?" "Everything's fine," I said, and played *The Holiday* on my Sky Box again; it's my go-to movie when I am feeling down.

I did eventually tell him this story, and I also told others too, and somehow it sounded funny when I said it out loud. I think the fact I didn't sugarcoat it – like I was really stabbing those cupcakes – made people feel better about themselves because ... guess what? Nearly every parent has had a cupcake moment or two.

Parenting was the first and main topic people wrote in about. It made sense because my Facebook page was originally about my struggles as a mom, and I probably shared more than most bloggers at the time, especially around the less "magical" sides of parenting and what it's like being a mom. What I have always found interesting though, and this is something I touched upon in my first book, is that even when confessing our secrets, even when remaining anonymous, people still struggle to push the boundaries and share their absolute truths about parenting.

You see, as mothers, it's socially acceptable for us to confess that sometimes motherhood is hard, that we don't enjoy every minute of it, that we steal our kids' snacks, skip pages in books, throw out their artwork and lie about the tooth fairy having a day off when we forget to leave money under our kids' pillows. It's even become sort of acceptable to say (behind their backs) that sometimes we wish they would just piss off or that they can, on occasion, be assholes. However, that's the limit. Moms are allowed to say they sometimes want a break from it all as long as they also follow it up with, "But I love them more than life itself and would never change a thing."

This is why so many of the mom confessions would end with the words "I feel so guilty" or "Does that make me a bad mother?" Only so often would I get a confession that would say "And I don't feel guilty at all". It's frustrating that there is still an expectation from mothers to either be perfect or, when we mess up, to at least feel guilty about it.

At the end of the day, and this I tell you after reading thousands of confessions from parents over the past five years, most of us fear the same things. We all make similar mistakes, the grass is nearly never greener on the other side, and you never know what's really going on with people behind closed doors.

When it comes to parenting there is so much shame and guilt; we've all grown up watching the same movie clichés after all. My idea of watching a lovely family film is all of us sitting together on one sofa, snuggled up with a blanket and eating popcorn out of one massive bowl. In reality, I have to give each kid their own bowl otherwise they'll kill each other, and I have to make sure they each get exactly the same amount of popcorn otherwise they might kill me! My image of bedtime stories also does not measure up. In movies it's calm, everyone is cosy in one bed and mom reads a lovely book with Cate Blanchett's voice. In fact, most nights I sound like the wicked witch as I bark orders: "Brush your teeth!", "Get a book!", "Will you get into bed!", while I collect their socks and dirty knickers off the carpet. When they finally agree on a book, they then start fighting over whose bed we should lie in. Honestly, I freaking hate bedtime. There's a confession for you.

I am sure there are people out there whose family life looks like those perfect Hollywood movies, but I am also sure I've just described most people's houses at bedtime. Don't worry, you're not alone, even if no one admits it openly.

When I went on tour, I had a whole section dedicated to "mom guilt" as part of my show. Each night I would share a mom-guilt-related confession. These were popular because there are very few mothers on the face of this planet who have never felt guilty about at least one thing relating to motherhood. But I always tried to share the stories of those who said they did not feel guilty, whatever fail they were confessing to. Why? Because they knew that it did not make them bad mothers. They knew that they were good mothers. They loved their kids with all their hearts, they were doing their best and that was more than enough.

Over the years the confessions started to change. Now I get all sorts – from regifting gifts to lying about kids' ages to get a free pass for Disney and, of course, a lot of dirty nappy confessions and revenge stories using breast milk. Yet as funny as many of them are, parenting has always been the one area that felt so important to discuss. I think it's because children challenge us in ways no high-powered job ever could; they remind us of our flaws, and the love we have for them can be, and often is, petrifying.

My favourite parenting confessions have always been parenting hacks. I love a parent that finds a way to make life a little easier. Why the hell not? A lot of parents lie about the ice cream van running out of ice cream when they don't want to get their kids an ice cream, screen time rules go out of the window on car trips, and one mom confessed that her way to make her kids behave on long flights was by giving them snacks every time they played up. My favourite parent hack of all times has to be the parent who taught their kid to cry on demand every time they stood in a long queue so that they would be allowed to go to the front of the line. Brilliant. I've never done that one. My kids would rat me out like they did that time I farted in the bank and all three of them yelled, "Mommy, yuck! Your fart stinks!" I wish I could go back to the days I could blame them for my gas – apparently all parents do!

In short, parenting – the emotions, the ups and downs, the joy and the sheer horror – are pretty universal. It honestly never mattered where the parents writing in were based, what culture or language they spoke. They all had one thing in common…They were all exhausted.

When my daughter was younger, about three, she was OBSESSED with Santa. Totally obsessed! Every two minutes she wanted to know where Santa was, who he lived with, what he was doing, eating for dinner . . . You get the idea.

One day, I had a terrible headache and I had had enough with the Santa questions all mother ducking day. I couldn't do it any more. I had calmly asked her several thousand times to change the subject. I tried so hard to redirect the conversation but no, we were still on the same subject. And it slipped out. Dear god, I wish it hadn't but it did. I snapped, "Santa is dead!"

She was confused because she didn't know what death meant. So I not only told my child that Santa was dead, but opened a new can of worms about what is "death".

———————————————————————— 41, Australia—

When I had my first child and reached the point of weaning, I was determined to do the best job ever. I'm talking baby-led weaning, plus all the homemade mash and pureed food you can imagine. My plan was to make big batches of it and freeze them. Honestly, I didn't know why I was doing it, I just felt I had to because of mom guilt and that sort of thing. By 8pm that evening I was in the kitchen surrounded by carrots, potatoes and veg everywhere – I was boiling and mashing over and over for hours.

At midnight I was a mess. There was mash potato everywhere, I was sweating like a pig and didn't even know what was what any more.

Suddenly I feel drops of water falling on my head. I look up and realize that, due to the steam and condensation, a lot of humidity had accumulated on my ceiling and it was now raining actual carrot juice in my kitchen.

That was my wake-up call – when you reach rock bottom and you suddenly realize what an absolute idiot you are. Needless to say,

I bought some Ella's Kitchen food after that and didn't bother with the homemade baby food.

39, Ireland

I am a doctor. I specialize in paediatrics and children, so when my five-year-old had an eye infection I knew exactly what it was and that I should probably keep her home and not send her to nursery because it's very contagious.

HOWEVER, I had a major meeting at work and could not afford to take the day off so, instead, I soaked her eye in eye drops and rolled up at nursery claiming she didn't have an eye infection but rather that we were using the drops as a prevention because there is an eye infection outburst. Obviously it was an awful lie, but they believed me because I am a doctor . . .

35, Israel

I'd had my first child and was up at all hours of the night breastfeeding while my partner (now ex) was fast asleep snoring his head off. One night I felt pure and utter rage toward him and toward the fact that I was so sleep deprived.

I finally put my daughter down in her crib, but she just wouldn't settle and he was still fast asleep snoring, so I sat bolt upright and turned around and slapped him around the face. Then I lay down and went back to sleep and let him deal with the baby seeing as he was now wide awake.

It was the best few hours of sleep I got and I felt so much calmer after. He wasn't happy with me at all but I genuinely didn't care.

31, UK

I am turning 35, married and have two kids – a daughter aged six and a son aged three. And I love my life. But right now it is just really hard. I guess I didn't imagine it all being this hard to do.

And at the same time I want more kids. Then I just keep thinking I'm craaaazy. Like, who would actually want more of this? But I do. Because at the end of the day, this is exactly what I asked for from life. Exactly what I longed for during that year that we couldn't get pregnant with my daughter, that year that we just wanted the dirty floors and dirty clothing and the exhaustion. Why is it that when you get what you want, you question ever wanting it?

But also I have this AMAZING husband that makes it all easier. So another few years and another few babies sounds fantastic by me. So yeah. That's my confession. I think I might be crazy but at least I have someone awesome to share the journey with. Oh, and we're in second lockdown in our country and we STILL don't want to get divorced.

———————————————————————————— 34, Israel

When my firstborn was around 18 months old, we went shopping for household bits and bobs. My daughter REALLY disliked her pushchair and insisted on walking most of the way round, which we thought ideal! We used her pushchair as a trolley, grabbed some things, placed them into the "trolley" and went to the till, paid for our things and walked out.

Our daughter was still refusing to go into her pushchair, and as we were walking to another store, the pushchair wheel got stuck in a little ditch and out flew a £30 blanket which I totally forgot I had placed where she would have been sat! It still had the security tag on, which didn't go off as we left the store.

Who knew toddlers were such great distractions that you could accidentally steal a £30 blanket?

———————————————————————————— 28, UK

When we don't want our kids to have playdates in our house because we would much rather our children go to other people's houses for a playdate, we lie and make up excuses and say, "We are having issues with the boiler and there will be a plumber in this afternoon so it's a bit hectic. Can Bella come round to yours today and next time we can host?"

Of course, next week the boiler is still not fixed and eventually people forget (or are too polite to say anything). Best parent hack ever.

— 40, Israel

I recently found out that I am pregnant with my fourth child. I'm still in shock and honestly I don't know what to do. I already thought about having an abortion but then the guilt takes over. I only think about the judgement of my family, my friends, my colleagues, everyone. I'm feeling so bad about it and lost.

— 38, Portugal

When my son got to about four he realized that Calpol tasted nice, and that if he said he needed medicine we would believe that he was sick in some way and that would score him time off school. So of course he started to say he needed medicine whenever he didn't want to go to school.

We realized that he didn't actually need it but he would lie through his teeth and you would always have that "but what if I'm wrong" thing at the back of your mind, so I took measures into my own hands. I told him, "Well, you can have medicine BUT you do realize that if you take medicine when you DON'T need it, your tongue will go purple and it will stay like that for a week and EVERYONE will know you lied about being sick." After that he never asked for medicine when he didn't need it again. He is now 12 and in secondary school and he STILL BELIEVES ME! He will to this day ask, "Is my tongue purple?" whenever he's not sure whether he jumped the gun a bit in taking medicine for something minor!

40, UK

When I was around six years old, I went to Morrisons supermarket with my parents. I was desperate for some sweets and asked if I could have some. Both Mum and Dad said no. I was upset and tantrummed. Which, of course, got a bigger no.

So I did the only thing I could think of. I stole a pack of Tic Tacs. The alarms didn't go off as we walked out with the packet in my pocket. I got home and gobbled them up but I felt so sick and I didn't know why.

I never told my parents as a child and I got away with it. The Tic Tac box sat in my toy box for years. I wouldn't let my mum throw it away and said I'd got it off a friend.

As a teenager I eventually fessed up to my mum. We lived across the country but that day she made me go to our nearest Morrisons and put the money for how much it would be in their charity donation pot. I was mortified when she told the lady at the till what I had done all those years before. Suffice to say I have never stolen anything since that day.

26, UK

Sometimes I really hate my kids. They are true demons raised from hell, and when they're truly annoying I lock them in their room so I can calmly drink my fucking cold coffee. They are two and six years old.

33, Slovenia

My kids and I went to an event in our small town downtown area called "Movie on the Square". My strong-willed, bull-headed daughter wanted to bring a friend and I didn't have it in me to argue, so I allowed it. We all got our special pyjamas on, pillows for the movie and headed out.

We had a great night, helped pick up trash after it was over and then headed off. When we got to the car, my middle daughter thought she'd show off to her friend by refusing to get in the car. After asking several times, and then everyone asking her to get in the fucking car, I said, "Fine, stay here!" I pulled out of the spot, backed up, did a "U-turn" in the parking lot and came back to where she was. But she wasn't there!

After searching for several minutes with no luck, my heart was pounding out of my chest and I called the police. The police came and I had to explain that "I didn't leave her, I was just trying to scare her, to get her to listen!"

After about an hour, an officer returns with my daughter, in her pyjamas, crying. I give her a hug and asked the officer where she was. As soon I'd backed up, she took off running downtown and they found her in her pyjamas with her pillow in one of the bars. As the police are telling me this, and I am still hugging her because I am still so happy to have her back, she whispers in my ear, "Don't play chicken with an 11-year-old. You raised me, and I will win!"

What the fuck have I raised . . . a fucking demon child?

36, US

My confession is about having a family. I kind of have the feeling I want to have kids, but I also have the feeling that I'll never be ready to give up sleeping till 10/11 on Sundays, and being free to do what I want when I want. I'm also so scared to get pregnant and suffer before, during and after birth. I know I'm still young, but yet there are

Parenting Confessions
29

some women that at 26 already have children, and I'm still buying Kinder Easter eggs because there is no Easter without them.

My friends feel like I do but sometimes I'm scared that, in spite of wanting them, I'm just too selfish and lazy to have children. I wonder sometimes how I could cope with the anxiety I'd mess them up or the fear of them getting hurt. I'm already soooo anxious.

— 26, Switzerland —

We had a hamster when the kids were little and when it died they wanted the full burial in the garden, but the ground was too dry to dig. So I told them not to worry, that I would find a way to dig that grave! When they were at school I made a cross out of lollipop sticks and wrote the hamster's name on it and stuck that in the ground (with difficulty) then er . . . wrapped him up and put him in the outside bin.

When the kids came home from school, I told them I'd managed to bury the hamster so we had the "ceremony" by the lollipop sticks!

51, UK

It was November and I got a really nasty cough that wouldn't budge and it was so difficult to recover with two hyper boys and a husband who tries to help . . .

A week later I was off to the doctor to be told it was pneumonia and would pass in a week, but I needed to wait for some swabs to come back to say whether or not I was contagious. My husband felt awful about his lack of support and for the first ever year offered to help with all the Christmas planning and watch the kids, so because I may have been contagious I snuggled in bed and watched Christmas movies while he did everything. Two days later I got the call from the doctor giving me the all clear . . .

I didn't tell my husband, of course, until after he had finished wrapping the Christmas presents and house cleaning. Best start to Christmas ever and my husband will never know.

26, UK

I pretend to be pregnant to get a seat on the tube, and when people don't give up their seat I give them "the look" – like what prick doesn't give their seat up for a pregnant woman? Usually other travellers nod and tut on my behalf until I get a seat. Sometimes being fat pays off.

36, UK

My toddler once grabbed hold of a top at Gap and I didn't pay for it because I hadn't noticed. When we left the store, I realized she was holding something. It was really nice and my size. I debated if I should go back and then decided not to because Gap is a big kahuna and I have spent a lot of money there. I felt like I deserved it.

The real confession is that I told my daughter about her "stealing" the top because I always thought it was funny she randomly picked something I liked and that fit me. One day she asked: "Mommy, did we actually steal it?" And I said, "No, sweetie. Mommy went back and paid for it later, obviously." I will take this lie to my grave.

I love my Gap top by the way, and wear it all the time.

41, UK

My youngest son, who was five at the time, gave me his tooth that had fallen out to look after. When bedtime arrived and he asked for it back so he could place it under his pillow, I didn't have the tooth and couldn't find it anywhere. So while I got him to look for it I quickly went upstairs and found my eldest son's old tooth which was still wrapped in tissue from ages ago . . . My son went to bed happy (but I felt guilty so I gave him an extra couple of pounds to make me feel better).

31, UK

A few hours after giving birth to my first child, I finally got her to stop screaming and must have dozed off while holding her, only to drop her head first off the hospital bed onto the floor.

Apart from a doctor I had to fess up to, it took hours before I told my husband and years before I ever told anyone else. In fact, almost nobody knows. Thankfully, she is a healthy eight-year-old girl now so I can look back and laugh.

31, UK

Being a mum is so hard sometimes! When my kids are being "annoying" (I mean little shits), I stick my fingers up and give them a "V" sign behind their backs because I just feel better afterwards.

32, UK

Two years ago my daughter had a birthday party and none of her classmates showed up. I don't know why exactly but NO ONE arrived. She was waiting with her little dress on, the house was decorated, the cake was ready but no friends!

My heart broke into a million pieces for her and I had to do something. So without her knowing, I rang the other mothers and cried my eyes out and begged them to bring their kids round, which they did. In the end there were quite a few children at the party and she never found out no one was planning to come. She just thought they were late.

— 32, Israel—

When my two children were little, we would lock them in their bedroom at night by putting a stick under the door handle so they couldn't get out. I would get a lot of surprised looks and a hefty dose of judgement for this but my reasons were simple . . .

One night we woke up at 1am and my eldest son had started running himself a bath – a scalding hot one. Luckily we found him before he had managed to climb in, but it was from this point that we started locking their door. My eldest could open child gates so that wasn't an option, and we were also worried about his brother following him in his escapades.

They are still alive now. Without third degree burns. So suck it.

— 33, UK—

When my girls really piss me off, I will calmly go to their sweet cupboard and systematically eat their sweets in front of them. I am going to hell.

— 35, UK—

During the Christmas holidays last year, every time we tried to get the kids out of the house, our nine-year-old refused to go anywhere as he wanted to spend the day on the PlayStation. Eventually I decided enough was enough, I turned off the power and told him there had been a power cut. I then faked a phone call to the electricity board, asking them when it would come back on and told him they had said it would be off until after teatime so we might as well go out. It worked like a charm!

We went out for the day and, after another fake phone call when we got back, the electricity was back on and he was happy as Larry. This trick came in handy on a number of occasions, including a few times when he refused to go to school and I convinced him that I would not be able to pay the bill for the power to come back on if I couldn't get to work.

37, UK

I was putting my toddler into the car seat, rushing to work as normal, when my daughter decided to do her usual push bum out of seat. I held her down firmly with one hand while putting the straps on (you all know the move) and she screamed all the way to nursery.

When I took her out of her seat I found a pink sippy cup under her bum! No wonder she couldn't sit down properly.

37, UK

My kids were fighting in the back of the car and I just lost my shit, pulled the car over, got out and sat at the side of the road saying that I wasn't getting back in!

40, UK

Once my son had a rather pompous friend over for a playdate. Coming up to lunchtime the friend came over to me while I was busy working/cruising the socials and tapped me on the shoulder saying, "I'd like my lunch now please. Cheese and cucumber on white bread with the crusts cut off." I was incredulous and a bit fierce.

Hatching a cunning plan, I warmed his sliced cheese up between my buttocks while using the cucumber slices as nipple eye coolers as I buttered the bread and cut off the crusts. He said, "Those were the most delicious sandwiches I've ever tasted."

Yes for butt cheek cheese! I had to leave the room for laughing.

46, UK

As a mum with a toddler, I did the big food shop with him being an utter little prick all the way round the store. As I was going through the checkout, I realized I hadn't picked up any grapes (his favourite) and my life would be hell without them. After I had finished at the checkout, I was so tired and stressed, I just went and picked up a punnet, put it in one of the bags and walked out. I couldn't face the checkout again.

47, UK

I told my middle son that I had found a foster family for him, just for a couple of weeks, so we could have respite. He was 13 and a real pain in the arse.

I elaborated that the family were close to his school so he would still see his friends and that they would keep a space for him so he could stay every few months if needed.

Terrible parenting and he still reminds me of it. Now he's a father and karma is the biggest bitch. His son is . . . let's say, challenging.

51, UK

Me and my husband recently had our second baby and one day he pissed me off so much I made him a milky coffee with breast milk! He still has no idea.

30, UK

Two months after my daughter's fourth birthday, and still with number 4 balloons in my house, I told my daughter that I'd opened the door and the balloons just flew out with the wind. They didn't, I couldn't take her bopping them in the air, at my face and around the TV any more so I took a kitchen knife to them (while she was at nursery – I'm not an animal).

However, my daughter got the last laugh as I hadn't realized they were filled with confetti! I'm still finding round circles of coloured paper.

30, UK

This is a hard one to write but I know that I am not alone, and that possibly other mums need to hear this . . .

When my first child was born it was not love, it was not natural, it was not Mother Earth – all those things that you assume. It was hard, so hard. It took a solid nine months (so basically my maternity leave) before I realized I loved him. By then I was leaving him. I suffered from postnatal depression, but never realized it till I had my second.

Now, most weeks I have at least two or three days still where I think I fucked him up, and I cry my heart out. He's nine in November!

I can honestly say I don't think I should have been a parent, but I wouldn't change it for the world. My babies complete me in a way I never knew possible, but it is harder than anyone could have impressed on me. The guilt is unbearable – I feel guilty right now writing this as my cooked-from-the-heart dinner is left on the table because "it's disgusting" and they are in the living room watching some crap on Netflix. Yeah, parenting is not easy for everyone.

———————————————————————— 41, UK—

I didn't bond with my son right away. It took me three months before I loved him unconditionally.

39, Canada

In lockdown my 23-year-old son grew a beard. One day he decided to shave it off, but his throwaway razors would not work on his beard. Being a helpful mum, I said I had a razor which would shave the beard off. I gave him said razor, and off he went.

He comes out of the bathroom a bit later telling me how fab my razor was. It's now sitting in a pot in the bathroom and he uses it all the time. But so do I – it's my bikini trimmer! Still not told him.

———————————————————————— 51, UK—

As we were driving with my family the other day, I got to thinking about life in general and, of course, death. My first thought was that I hope my children have happy memories of me when I go. And then I felt sad because I realized that when my dad passes away, I am not sure how sad I will be. I feel bad for feeling that way and also a little sad at how little our relationship means to me. I see how my husband is with our children and it makes me so happy and makes me realize how a father should be for his children – their hero, rock and biggest cheerleader.

———————————————————— 40, Cyprus—

When my youngest was two and I was pregnant with my second, my husband and I would often have a bowl of ice cream in the evening after my daughter was in bed.

We live in a small ranch-style house with barely any insulation, so she began to recognize the sound of spoons in bowls. She would come out as soon as she heard the clinking sound and we would rush to hide our bowls of ice cream under blankets, couch cushions, books and even under our shirts. It became a competition to eat without our spoons touching the bowl; whoever made the first sound obviously lost and had to take her back to bed. We even got so desperate as to eat with wooden cooking spoons and bought plastic spoons specifically for our ice cream eating. Anything to avoid having to share it with her!

36, US

One night while putting my two-year-old son to bed, he was being a crazy person and running around and kept getting out of bed. He thought it was the funniest thing ever and would laugh and laugh each time I put him back. So one of the times he got out of bed I waited in the hallway. I was at the end of my rope, tired and over it, so when he ran into the hallway and headed toward the living room, I yelled out, "There are monsters in there!" Needless to say, that worked and he ran back to bed. But then he started crying and was terrified, so this was both a parenting win and fail. He was in bed but I might have scarred him for life.

35, US

When my son was 14 years old, he and his buddy decided that they would commit vandalism at a nearby trucking lot – smashing windows and what not. They were spotted on video and it was posted on Facebook by the local authorities. I saw it while I was at work, left work and picked him up and turned him in to the police. He had to do community service but the owners did drop the charges. So yeah – I turned my own kid in to the police.

39, US

My son is two and he sleeps on his stomach. Yes, so that means a lot of pee – pee all over him, his jammies and his sheets every single fucking morning. He is soaked on a daily basis when he wakes up. I double diaper him and even use an incontinence pad but NOTHING stops the never-ending river of piss from soaking him. So morning after morning I get my sweet pee-boy, march him into the bath and trudge back to change his sheets for the millionth time. Well, last week I just couldn't face it, with an insane amount of work deadlines, caring for my son alone, a puppy with diarrhoea and working on about two hours' sleep. I decided, "Fuck it, pee is sterile. Right?" I baby wiped my kid down, and set the fan toward the bed to dry the piss up naturally. I felt badly about it but even worse when it came to naptime and the bed wasn't dry. Did I change the sheets then? Nope, I threw two towels across the length of the mattress and laid my son on top.

40, US

I told my son I'm allergic to play dough so I don't have to play with that god-awful stuff. He believes me and makes sure he doesn't leave a mess behind so I don't accidentally touch it. I'm not allergic to anything.

27, US

I found weed in my 18-year-old's room so I took his car keys for one week and lectured him. I took the weed with me on a moms' weekend and we had a fabulous weekend smoking his weed!

42, US

My son was seven and we went to my mom's while she was at work to pick something up. I kept telling him it was time to go. He kept saying okay but was still digging in his toy box that he played with when he visited. He thought it was funny that I was getting irate so I told him I was going.

He was still giggling as I walked out of the door. I got in the car and drove to the neighbour's house about a block away (on a gravel road with no traffic). I waited there about three minutes and drove back to my mom's to find my son carrying a dump truck toy and sobbing as he walked down the road toward me. I couldn't help laughing at him as he got into the car still crying. I asked him where he was going. He said he was walking home. I just laughed harder because home was 7 miles away. I know I'm awful. However, he was always the first one in the car after that.

47, US

My son was born nine weeks early so I had to have him by emergency C-section. The breastfeeding nurse came to speak to me the next day and was talking to me and my boyfriend about nipple stimulation and she told my partner to rub my nipples to stimulate my milk flow. Obviously one thing led to another and we ended up having sex in hospital the day after a C-section. Oops.

28, Afghanistan

My grown-up son had a friend that would ALWAYS help himself to everything in the kitchen, was always too broke to pitch in for pizza, etc, but would eat the most and had lots of money for himself every other time. So I prepared Ex-Lax (laxative) chocolate cupcakes just for him.

52, US

I had a selection of sex toys I kept in a large shoe box. When we moved house I sealed the box with tape so it couldn't fall open. I forgot about this when I put the shoe boxes away and there it sat on top of my cupboard.

 I searched the loft for this box, thinking I was looking for an ordinary packing box, and eventually reasoned it must have got lost.

 About six months later I had a clear-out of the 40+ boxes of shoes I had, thinking "I don't need this many", so I decided to donate about 10 pairs.

 It wasn't until I was lying in bed a few nights later that it suddenly dawned on me where my special box was. Imagine their faces at the charity store opening a box of vibrators, nipple and clit stimulators and all sorts of other things!

50, UK

Is it just me or is it easier to just pleasure myself? With shift patterns and five children aged from 3 to 14, there is no time and no privacy . . . We're like ships passing.

36, UK

I smoke weed. My kids go to bed and I smoke weed to calm down. I have eight kids and they drive me nuts. I am a single parent – can you blame me?

— 33, US —

My boyfriend and I were helping his mother move house and she asked me if I could pack her clothes. "Sure," I said, though this was the beginning of my relationship with this guy so we did not know each other's family that well.

After packing a few boxes, I felt something long and very hard at the back of the cupboard. Wondering what this could be, I take it out and it was the biggest black dildo I had ever seen . . . with a strap-on belt! I was so shocked and amazed that this older lady had this in her cupboard.

At that moment my boyfriend and his mother walked in. He was shocked and she was embarrassed. Trying to make the situation better, I said it was mine! That I was going to a hen night and this was the present for my friend.

The look of relief on my boyfriend's mum's face was huge. She was so thankful and we are still friends to this day.

— 24, Bolivia —

I have an eight-year-old autistic daughter and we sleep in the same bed. My husband gets annoyed and he thinks I should sleep train her. I always tell him I feel bad to have her sleep alone, and I do, but the reality is he is the worst person to sleep with. He snores, moves a lot and has to have the TV on. So I'm never going to sleep with him, or tell him, because I don't want to hurt his feelings.

— 36, US —

One night I wanted to have a thrilling one-night stand but had kids and couldn't get a babysitter. Out of respect for my kids, I don't allow hook-ups in my house when they are home. The guy came over and was ready to come in, but I said, "Sorry, not today as the kids are asleep." He looked at me confused and then I pointed to the bonnet of his car.

Let's just say that the seedy neighbour had a peek and listen while we silently laughed and had the best "back to 18" sex ever!

38, Australia

My son had lost his tooth and I had totally forgotten about tooth fairy duty. When he brought it up three days later, we told him she was really busy but she would definitely be there that night. The night comes and he finally goes to sleep. Unfortunately, we had absolutely no change whatsoever so we took the money out of his piggy bank and put it under his pillow.

32, UK

In August I made a long-awaited trip back home. I've been living on the US East Coast for 12 years and the West Coast has been calling me back. On the trip back home, I made a major mistake – I had sex with my ex-husband. I've been happily remarried for seven years and estranged from said ex for ten years while co-parenting one amazing twelve-year-old.

Well, I came home with a gift. I am pregnant, and I'm certain it's not with my current spouse.

35, US

I have identical twin boys. When I got them home from hospital, I realized I could not tell them apart so didn't remove their hospital ID. After a week I realized they wouldn't be able to keep them on for life! I stripped them naked and looked everywhere for a birth mark to distinguish them. Nothing! Not even under their willies or between their butt cheeks! I ended up painting pink nail varnish on one of the twin's big toes so I knew them apart!

50, UK

Some days I feel that having three kids was too much, and I feel guilty about it because they also made me the woman I am today.

For example, today my eldest wanted me to show her how to shave and had an attitude all day because I said no (she's only ten). Meanwhile, my middle son decided he should now learn how to clean himself when he takes a shit and so his hands were all covered, of course. And my baby is now two and does not speak a word and cries all day! Of course, dealing with the baby's daddy is a whole other level.

I just need a break and can't tell anyone about it.

26, Costa Rica

Lockdown began to get way too much – the constant noise, mess and never being able to pee in peace. I have three children in my house, my two boys and my husband. My husband decided lockdown was his opportunity to relive his youth and teach our sons some practical jokes, so every day turned into fart machines and fake poops. However, my eldest didn't understand what was fake and what was real so started leaving actual poop! So I did what any semi-sane woman would do when you aren't allowed to go out in a lockdown to get away from the three disgusting children. I went shopping . . .

I told my husband I needed to go and do the food shop. Little did he know it was a Click and Collect, so I collected the shopping, parked round the corner and did some retail therapy on my phone in my car. One day I even pulled up and just napped!

I told my kids the Christmas Elf was naughty because they can't behave. Now my five-year-old has terrifying nightmares about the Elf every night.

I am a single parent who is no longer in touch with any blood relatives, and I was having a lockdown baby in May. Friends kept offering to come to the hospital with me when I went into labour, as they didn't want me to be alone but, in all honesty, I wanted to be by myself for it. Not because of COVID, but I chose to have the little one as a single parent so wanted to have that experience without distractions from anyone else.

In the early hours of the morning my waters went, so I rang my eldest's grandma to pick him up (she is a saint). I drove myself to hospital in between contractions, but didn't call any of my friends who had offered to come with me. The little one arrived within an hour of being in the hospital. I told each of my friends that I didn't call them as it was early and the midwife said I was going to get checked over and then sent home to labour, at which point I would have called them.

I probably should have told them the truth, but each of them felt like they were doing me a huge favour and I didn't want to take that away from them.

I sometimes forget to brush my toddler's teeth. I am not sure why it's so hard for me to remember, but it's a good thing that these teeth will fall out.

29, UK

My now husband took me to a beautiful cabin in the mountains for my birthday, it was the first time we said "I love you". A few months later, he proposed. Well, a few weeks after the proposal, we found out we were pregnant. We decided to get married on New Year's Eve at the mountains where we first declared our love. Our son was five months old at the time.

After saying "I do", we drove to our honeymoon destination, which was another cabin in the woods. When we arrived at our romantic getaway spot, my husband went to check us in and my son woke up. I pulled him out of his car seat and pulled down his pants to check his diaper and he shit ALL OVER ME. I swear to god, it was all over my dress and my shoes and probably even in my hair. Even our poor dog was covered in poo.

Needless to say, the first thing I did when we checked into our cabin was to take a long shower and burn my wedding dress. If this story doesn't explain what motherhood and marriage is all about, I don't know what does.

43, US

My mum was super mean and told me that the ice cream van that I could hear going up and down the road was in fact a mobile disco and I would dance my little heart out every time I heard it. My cousin ruined my mum's fun by telling me the truth when I was about four.

Her other story was about the hair fairy. (Yes, you read that right.) I was terrified of having my hair cut as I always thought it was going to hurt, so my mum invented the hair fairy who would take the last lock of hair cut from my head and, much like the tooth fairy, would leave money under my pillow in replacement. Seriously, what was I thinking?

I struggled with my mental health before I had my daughter. After the birth I moved into a place with just me and her and it got a lot worse.

One night I remember being in the kitchen and my daughter was in bed. I think I was making a sandwich and I was having a really bad day with my depression. I was holding the knife to my wrist and sobbing. Suddenly my daughter started crying and it was like coming out of a trance. I dropped the knife and went and cuddled her. If it wasn't for my daughter, I may not be here to write this.

Motherhood is having three cups of coffee in the morning, only to RACE home from the park at lunchtime while pinching your knees together so as not to pee your pants.

And making it! Only to see the toilet and then your bladder releases a little urine in your pants to celebrate.

Once, when things were tight moneywise, I had £20 left over for the weekend until I got paid on the Monday. However, two of my daughters came home from school with nits so off I went to the chemist with my last bit of cash. I bought the de-nitting lotion, took it home and sorted out the kids' hair. Then despicable me re-filled the bottles that I purchased from the chemist with some cheap moisturizer and got the refund from the store. It was a bit naughty but the things you do to get by . . .

— 45, UK

I found out I was pregnant when I was 19. I wasn't dating anyone at the time and had slept with two different guys. I had chosen to date the one I had slept with most recently, but he ended up being abusive. I was so scared to have a baby with him that I looked up ways to cause a miscarriage. I'm pro-choice, but I knew my family would be angry at me for getting an abortion. My boyfriend found out, which obviously caused issues, and my attempts failed.

Now I have a beautiful three-year-old boy, plus my fiancé and I have two other boys. But I've never told anyone I tried to cause a miscarriage with my first pregnancy.

— 23, US

I love my kids but I wish I didn't have any.

40, US

I'd been on full-time mum duty since March – thanks, COVID – then my children went back to school for a few days then were off school due to me showing symptoms (I was negative in the end). A cough and cold then hit our house, cue the kids being off again. They got better so they went back to school again.

I was thinking "Great", and planning all the things I was now going to do but no . . . I got a phone call on the Monday evening telling me one of my children had been in contact with a positive case of COVID, so he was off and isolating for two weeks. Which obviously meant I was stuck home.

So for the last two days, I've quit! I've done absolutely nothing but feed said child and sit watching TV. I've told my partner when he comes home from work that I've not felt well – you know, headaches, period pains and a bad back. I'm actually feeling fine , just can't be arsed to do anything in the house right now. Bad mum or genius [evil laugh]?

— 34, UK

I am an only parent (widowed for nine years) of a ten-year-old. I work six days a week. But once a month I take a day off mid-week to spend all day in bed at my boyfriend's house.

— 40, US

On a particularly tiring day during the first Scottish lockdown in 2020, the clock struck 5pm and I'd had enough. I was exhausted, the house was a mess and my four-year-old had just dropped his dinner plate on the floor. Ketchup stained (still stains) the carpet and the dog was balls deep in chicken goujons and potatoes, living his best life. My tolerance threshold was but a mere flicker in the rear-view mirror and I was losing my shit. So I changed the clocks. I changed all the clocks that my son would see. Instead of 5pm, it was now 7pm, and that meant bedtime. My son questioned me, knowing he had only just had dinner and that daylight still brightened his room, but when I pointed out the time, how could he argue? It was indeed bedtime.

We skipped the bath, got pyjamas on, I grabbed the shortest bedtime story from the bookcase, then kiss, cuddles, lights out . . . Freedom. Totally worth it. I would do it again.

30, UK

Sometimes when I feel overwhelmed at home, I'll hide something in the kitchen and tell my husband we are out of it so I have a reason to go to the store. There I cry in the parking lot before I go in or I'll swing by the daiquiri store and down a frozen daiquiri before going on to the store.

31, US

I was putting my son's socks away one day when he was about 13 and I found an open box of condoms. After discussing what to do with my best friend, whose daughter had also started having sex at a very young age, I decided to simply buy him a box in bulk from Amazon. I didn't want there to be any "oopsies" at 13. I kept an eye on the box, and when it was almost empty I ordered another.

A scary thing happened, though. Thank goodness his girlfriend was (maybe) on birth control because one night, they came out of his bedroom and my son said very seriously that they needed to get to the pharmacy RIGHT AWAY. Apparently the condom had slipped off his penis while he was still inside her. They needed a "Plan B" pill – the morning after pill. I drove to five different pharmacies before I could find one that was open.

My son paid for the pill and then they began to discuss how to get the condom out – it was still inside her! I explained to her how to do it, and my son was very uncomfortable, "Do we have to talk about this?" At which his girlfriend shot him a nasty look and said, "Don't you think we're beyond embarrassment at this point?"

It all turned out okay in the end. He's 18 and in college now . . . and can buy his own damn condoms.

My husband has slept on the couch since 2010. Yes, you read that correctly. Ten years of sleeping on the couch. Why? First, when I was pregnant, the smell of the Biofreeze I used for my carpel tunnel made my husband gag. Then the baby was born and we co-slept. Then his snoring and god-awful alarm tone kept the baby and I awake. He is usually a trouper about it; but sometimes he gets pissed. And I, only sometimes, feel guilty.

I love my husband. Really. But god, do I love my sleep more than anything else.

So we have a 19-month-old boy who has been sleeping through the night for about five months now. But it's a secret – my husband doesn't know!

I wake hubby up at 5am every morning and say I had an awful night with the bubba – and hurray, he sends me to bed, organizes the kids and makes me a cup of coffee that I am woken up with after he drops off the kids at childcare.

I heard him crying to himself this morning that he is so tired.

It was a difficult day. Then you know that moment your child is having a meltdown and you're running out of ideas and you can't stop yelling? So I said, "Come on, stop kicking off or . . . errrr . . ."

I turned around and grabbed the first things in sight – a Mayor Goodway Paw Patrol model and a stove gas lighter – the clicky flame thing – and said as I held the flame near Mayor Goodway. "I'll . . . er, I'll . . ." And then Whoooosh. Up she went like a Roman candle. Oops.

From now on, all I have to say is "Remember what happened to Mayor Goodway? Do you want that to happen again?"

#mumoftheyear #traumaforlife

— 46, UK

I only breastfeed my babies because I'm cheap and extremely lazy. Cheap because I won't pay for formula, lazy because I don't have to wash a single dish. It's an excuse for me to lay down and I get to hide from my other kids because the baby needs "quiet". Also my husband brings me water and snacks.

— 33, US

We are remote learning/home schooling. My selfless reason for doing it was to protect my kids and to free up the space for other families that have to send kids to school. But my real reason for keeping them home is so I don't have to piss around trying to wake them up every morning and worry about lunches.

— 50, Canada

Revenge and In The Office Confessions

I have never ever told anyone (except my husband Mike) about this and I can't believe I'm actually confessing this because, let's face it, it's vandalism ... but here goes! When I was 22 and still living in Israel, one afternoon I drove to the mall with my then boyfriend and younger sister. It was a Friday afternoon, which meant the mall was busy, everyone was frantically getting their food shopping or their hair and nails done before the weekend. Like most Fridays, finding a good parking space was a challenge. I had already circled the car park several times when I spotted a car reversing out of a spot, so I quickly drove up and positioned my car right by the spot, waiting for them to drive off.

As the car reversed out slowly, a second car appeared out of nowhere, accelerated and, before I knew it, drove straight into MY parking space.

I was furious.

It was clearly my spot so I decided to confront the driver. I stepped out of my car and walked toward the other vehicle. At this point the driver from the other car got out of the car – it was an older woman, she must have been in her forties, and she was very tall, much taller than me. She walked toward me with determination and a smile. I was saying something like, "Hey, that's my space, I've been waiting for it," but before I could even finish my sentence she had reached me. She lifted her hand and swung her entire arm and slapped me right across the face. I literally went flying. I remember my shock so clearly even 20 years later.

Then she laughed and walked away, heading into the mall. I stood there, unable to move, my hand on my cheek, trying to make sense of what just happened. This woman hit me in broad daylight over a parking space at the mall.

All I recall is looking back at my own car and seeing my boyfriend's and sister's faces staring at me in utter disbelief. They were so shocked they didn't even come to my help, they just sat there with their mouths open.

You're probably wondering what is the confession in all of this. Well, here it comes. After the shock wore off, I was so angry and I wanted revenge, so I walked up to her car, took out my house key and I keyed her entire car from one end to the other. I'm pretty sure I even wrote some nasty message on her bonnet with my key. After that we left fast before anyone saw us. It felt so good!

However, I've always looked back at that event and felt slightly guilty about it. Until I read other people's revenge stories and realized that keying a car is not as vindictive as some of the other things people do to get back at those who cross them.

The classic has to be the toothbrush in the toilet routine. Wow! Chilli powder and other stinging ointments on balls and penises are also rather popular. One woman who was really dedicated washed her boyfriend's underwear in wasabi water after she found out he had cheated on her. Lots of people end up at the emergency room convinced they have some rare skin condition. And let's not forget laxatives in coffees as another great move to get back at someone.

I love revenge stories. I know I shouldn't because most of them involve someone either drinking wee or using cutlery that someone else farted on or had between their butt cheeks, but usually the revenge is for a good reason so it sort of makes it okay. Sort of.

The two main crimes that incite revenge are either cheating or being a nasty boss. And who hasn't had a nasty boss they wanted to get back at? I know I have. So be nice to your employees because you never know what they've put in your tea (usually spit or sweat) or what they've washed your favourite mug in. (Yes, you guessed it – toilet water.)

Weirdly, I have no great revenge stories from the workplace. I have, however, had a few funny experiences. When I first came to London in 2006, I worked at a swanky central London restaurant as a hostess. For the three months I worked there, my boss consistently called me "Yoda", thinking that was actually my name. I never corrected him. I would just sit there at the staff meeting and let him say stuff like, "Yoda, today you'll be doing the bookings," or, "Where is Yoda?" Or my favourite, "If you have any questions, just ask Yoda." It took a lot of effort not to pee myself laughing, but I would somehow maintain a straight face and nod in an all-knowing way. After all, I was "Yoda".

When it comes to work-related stories, do I confess to the amount of lies I have told on my CV? I feel like everyone does that, right? I think most people "embellish" their CVs. I remember when I was trying to make my way as a young actress and auditions were hard to come by, so when someone said they were looking for an actress who could speak French, I applied for the job thinking I could wing it. For the record, I did live in Paris for six months in my early twenties and at the time I could almost get by, but my acting days came over a decade later and at that point my French was completely useless. I figured they would want to see me first, and then, if I made it to the next round, I would get some text in French to learn and prepare in advance so it would be fine. Famous last words.

After the initial hellos and usual questions you'd get asked in a casting, the director handed me a script that was completely in French and asked me to read the role of Sophie – a French teacher who was on the run from the police because of a mistaken identity.

Shit. Or should I say "merde"?

The way I saw it, I could either admit I had totally lied about how well I spoke French. OR I could dig an even deeper hole for myself and keep lying. Naturally I chose the latter. I said I was a fluent speaker but not great at reading and that if they gave me time to prepare with the text I would be able to nail it.

The director's reply was, "Don't worry, we just want to hear a few lines. That's all. No worries if it's not perfect."

So I read the script – like a four-year-old sounding out the letters in phonics, not knowing what any of what I was reading even meant, and not looking up as the room suddenly became completely silent and tense. Someone once told me that if you do things with confidence, you can get away with almost anything. It clearly doesn't work when you're faking being able to speak French. I was getting warmer and warmer, my cheeks were turning red but there was no going back now. I had to get to the end of the paragraph, no matter what. When I finished there was a long silence. It was as if someone had just let go of a bad fart that was hanging in the air, but no one wanted to be the first to say anything because everyone was still a little traumatized.

Eventually I just stood up and said, "So you'll call me?" and ran.

Needless to say, they never called.

After that experience I took French off my CV and I never told anyone this story … until now.

I collected some dog poo (not from my dog – I don't have one) and smeared it under the door handles of my ex's car. I only wish I'd been there to witness him find it.

I once cleaned my bathroom and toilet with my soon-to-be ex-husband's toothbrush. His mum gave me the idea when she found out he was sleeping around like his dad did.

My mother-in-law always thinks she's right, and gets insanely jealous over my own mum. Over the years I've let her nasty comments slide and not argued back when I easily could have, but during the summer I made my mum a cheesecake and the mother-in-law made a comment over it, acting like I don't do anything for her. So I surprised her with the same type of cheesecake. She was pleased. What she didn't know was that I spat in it several times as revenge for her nasty ways.

I knew only she would be eating it, so each slice was eaten by her greedy self.

I used to study catering at college and there was this one guy in our class who used to act like the best and constantly brag about his life and test scores, and would take the piss out of other people if they didn't know how to cook something. It got to the point where everyone had had enough, and one day he left his workstation to go and get some more ingredients and so I decided to use that time to put chilli powder in all of his dishes. He also had a pot of paprika on his station so I tipped most of it out and topped it back up with chilli powder, then mixed it so he wouldn't know the difference. When he came back he added some of the contents of his paprika pot (now chilli powder) into his dishes and served it to our teacher for evaluating. He didn't taste any of his dishes before serving them. The teacher tried the first dish and spat it out saying, "Are you trying to blow my head off? This dish is not supposed to be spicy. You were told to follow the recipe, not change it."

My now ex went out with a friend one night to a gig and then for a few drinks afterwards, saying he wouldn't be later than 12.30. The time came and went so I double-locked our front door, left the keys in the back of the door and refused to let him in. He had to spend the night sleeping in the car.

I should add he had a job interview the next day and needed a good rest. It didn't happen because he was late and I locked him out. Ever since then he's never been late to do anything with me again!

My brother's girlfriend was living with us. She was so controlling, vindictive and spiteful and was always starting fights. So I decided that, being the wonderful future sister-in-law I am, I would start cooking for everyone. She hated any kind of vegetables so very kindly I would make her a separate batch of food to everyone else and I would add my secret ingredient to her batch: *weight gain powder*. She put on about two stone in a month.

One time my friend was having trouble with a colleague – the boss's mistress – at work. She thought that as she was screwing him she ran the place. So we decided to get back at her.

We made a penis cake and sent it to her. We included penis plates, penis forks, penis lollipops, penis napkins and condoms wrapped like penises, with balloons that said Happy Birthday. Then we paid a friend of ours to deliver it in the middle of the busiest time of day. It really was her birthday.

We made sure you couldn't see anything in the box till it was all the way open. My friend was standing right next to her when she opened it and acted all shocked. The colleague knew who'd sent it but could never prove it.

She told my friend she didn't know she was like that and how inappropriate it was for the workplace. Just as the boss walked by. He heard and the colleague got in trouble. He didn't fire her but she no longer held any positions of power, in or out of the bedroom.

—————————————————————————————————————— 41, US—

When me and my ex split up, I signed his name, email address and cellphone number up to every gay dating site/hook-up site I could find. He was the biggest homophobe you could come across.

——————————————————————————————————————— 31, UK—

My sister's partner left her for another woman, but he insisted on taking the new cheese grater with him. So before he collected it, she grated the corn on her foot with it and peed on it, then shoved it in a carrier bag and left it on the front doorstep. He collected it and off he went to his new girlfriend's house!

——————————————————————————————————————— 32, UK—

When my nan discovered my grandad was having an affair, she decided not to confront him but to get revenge.

One night when he came home from work, he sat down to a "delicious" homemade meal of pie, mashed potatoes and peas. After consuming said meal, my nan asked how he liked his food and enjoyed breaking the news that the pie filling was in fact dog food!

— 33, UK

I'm a teacher, and when marking my primary grade kids on their weekly assignments, I sometimes give the average of the previous scores when I have forgotten to note a kid's marks in my teacher's diary.

27, India

I used to work in a small hardware store years ago. Often there would only be three of us closing, along with the manager. There was this one male co-worker who was insanely attractive and, more importantly, his smell drove me insane!

After a while we started having sex at work and one night, right after closing, we snuck off to the warehouse to have sex. It was great by the way. When we were done we went back to work, but unknown to us the third co-worker had had to leave and our boss had been looking for us for about 20 minutes. He asked where we had been and we didn't really have a good answer . . . but man did I sleep good that night.

— 35, US

When my husband and I moved into our first house, we needed to purchase a new bed, so I bought a second-hand one off a local site who said they could deliver it for us. When they arrived I went outside to help carry in the divan base, which needed two people as it was light but bulky. The middle-aged man instantly asked if my husband was available to help. I was so annoyed with him for assuming I couldn't help that I just said, "Sorry, my wife is at work." This led to a sheepish look and then much conversation asking what she did and how did we meet and so on as I helped carry in the bed.

After this pleasant chat, he went to leave but first he took my hand in his and said, "Sorry for earlier. I am gay myself. I hope you have a happy life together." Then he left, with me feeling terrible for lying to him.

35, UK

When I was with my ex he had a very weird relationship with his mother, and all I heard was how his mother did a better job than I did. He even once told me he heard his mum and dad having sex for over an hour, and I should have more stamina like her! As you can imagine this was the ultimate cause for the end of our relationship.

So one evening, when he got in from work, I made meatballs and pasta, and of course got told his mum's are so much better blah blah blah. By this point I was good at ignoring him. The following day he tells me his mum and dad were coming over for dinner, and I'd better cook something nice, not the mess I cooked last night as he wouldn't even feed it to our dog. I was fuming. But the idea of a dog's dinner left me with an idea . . .

As his mum and dad were sat eating dinner, his mum commented that the meatballs were delicious, more juicy than ever and she was impressed how the centre was chunked meat. I smiled like a Cheshire cat. My boyfriend told me it's the best thing I have ever cooked and he was so pleased I had given meatballs another try, especially after how bad last night's were. I obviously didn't eat the meal.

After they left my boyfriend goes on about how rude I was not to eat, and how I must have bought the meatballs from a restaurant and he demanded to know what was in them.

I very calmly grabbed my overnight bag, filled it with my things and, as I left, told him all the ingredients were on the side. Halfway down the street I got a text demanding I tell him it wasn't true! That the can of dog food on which I put a post-it note reading "meatball surprise" was a joke. I just laughed and told him he best go to his mum and she will make it all better, and never spoke to him again.

Sometimes revenge really is necessary! And it's okay to feel so sweet!

26, UK

My ex-husband was always cheating in some way – with cyber or actual friends. So I decided to have revenge of my own, and had sex with an old fuck buddy of mine in the chair my ex-husband liked to use in the evenings for his work. He still doesn't know to this day.

34, UK

My sister had decided her long-term boyfriend was going nowhere, so she put on a whole big show to our parents that he was abusive, etc, so they would rescue her and let her move in (she admitted it to me). This obviously got out and painted this guy in a horrendous light. She then proceeded to go on a load of dates with various guys, getting free nights out and still being utterly doted on by our parents. She was always the golden child who was given a house, money, cars, etc.

One day I'd had enough of her playing the princess, so went into her emails and forwarded all the rather graphic seedy sext emails (minus contact details) that she'd been sending to THREE guys to our parents and to the guys.

An hour later I felt guilty though, and deleted it from our parents account so they never knew. She got a huge fright though, and had no more free meals or treats.

My mum passed away suddenly when I was 21. I took two weeks off work but my head was in such a spin that I hadn't even thought about getting a sick note or phoning in (bar phoning to tell them what had happened).

One of the directors instructed my line manager to contact me the following week and ask for my resignation if I hadn't been in contact. She was horrified so she secretly phoned me to tell me to phone in quickly, as if I'd just done it myself. I got myself in such a tizz that I just went straight back to work in case I lost my job.

Anyway, confession . . . At the next board meeting I was preparing the tea and coffee for the directors and I noticed that no one had cleaned out the coffee percolator after the last meeting, and the old coffee had gone mouldy in the filter.

So I spooned in the required amount of coffee ON TOP OF THE MOULDY STUFF, gave it a stir and switched that sucker on.

I was also responsible for pouring the tea and coffee so the directors that were good to me got told the coffee wasn't the best and given tea. The rest of them got multiple cups.

After my partner had an affair he begged and begged for a second chance but that wasn't happening. At the time we still had to live together until I sorted a new home out for me and the kids. I was absolutely furious that he had destroyed our family and the 20 years we had spent together, so every day I would clean the toilet with his toothbrush and I rubbed the hottest ghost chilli into the seams on the groin area of all his jeans, knowing he always goes commando and very rarely washes his jeans.

He came to me late one night after he had been for a few drinks with his mates to say he was sorry to bother me but didn't know where else to go but that he needed help getting an STD (sexually transmitted disease) check as his balls had been on fire and were so itchy he was convinced he had caught something. I passed him some cream to calm the area, which happened to be Vicks VapoRub, and the scream that came out of the bathroom literally made my revenge complete. I have never told him that I was rubbing the chilli into his jeans and he thinks I had passed him the VapoRub as an accident because he woke me up from my sleep. Needless to say the nurse at the STD clinic had a good giggle at him walking into the clinic like John Wayne and smelling like his backside had a cold.

— 41, UK

So my husband and I have been married for 19 years and I had decided to spice things up. While I was at home I decided I would take some naughty down-below pictures, not knowing he was showing his 25-year-old employee something on his phone when my inappropriate picture came through as a text message. His employee just turned away mortified. (You'd think I would've learned after I accidentally sent the paediatrician a picture of my boobs when I was trying to send him a picture of my son's rash.)

— 40, US

When my kids were small I would sometimes throw a sickie at work just to get a day to myself. I would then spend the whole day feeling guilty and race to get the kids from nursery at the end of the day.

44, UK

At the age of 32, after a 16-year relationship, I was suddenly single and back out there in the big wide world. I started dating someone I had known from school when I was a teenager. I didn't expect it to be anything serious, but I wasn't seeing anyone else and I did make an effort. After a few months, a friend sent me a photo of a dating site showing this said man advertising himself. I was mortified – we hadn't made promises but said we were exclusive. So I asked him outright, and his reply was, "No harm looking for the next better bird – always on the market for an upgrade." I was livid!

So I plotted my revenge. I invited him over for cooked spaghetti Bolognese and ground up my toenail clippings . . .

He ate the lot then assumed he was in for some sexy time, so I told him to fuck off and leave.

46, UK

I once lived with a nasty boyfriend who complained that I didn't put enough pepper in his egg sandwich. So I dried out some hamster poo and chopped it into tiny pieces. He said it was delicious. Revenge is sweet!

59, Canada

Me and my ex had had words, but I was kind and said I'd still make him his lunch. I buttered some bread but then the phone rang so I left the kitchen. While on the phone, I turned around and saw my cat was sat on one of the buttered slices and was licking the other one.

I finished my call and went into the kitchen, lifted the cat down, put some ham onto the bread and got the cat to lick the ham, then put the bread together and gave him his sandwich for work.

He said they were nice. Ha!

48, UK

I was knocked up by what turned out to be the worst excuse for a human being. Along with violence and alcohol abuse, he also had a gambling problem. (Which is problematic when you owe child support – not for my daughter, I never asked for it, but on his other five kids.)

One day he showed up at my house, not to see his daughter, but to beg me to cash a $1,000 winning lottery ticket. He went with me to get the payout for the ticket, which was paid to me in a cheque in my name. He then went with me to the bank to get the cheque cashed. He was too busy complaining about everything to notice I filled out the bank slip to deposit $750 and cash $250. I told him there were fees for cashing a cheque that size.

Yes he protested. I told him this was a small price to pay considering the entire amount would have been seized if the payout had been in his name.

I honestly don't know how he didn't figure it out.

38, US

I had been working from home since March and I needed to go to a first aid course for work, over an hour away. A work colleague (who makes me want to slam my head into the keyboard or backslap them across their head) asked if they could have a lift. I told said person that "I was currently isolating and didn't want to risk them catching it". In fact I'm fine, I just didn't want to have to push them out of the car halfway and get done for assault and reckless driving. One good thing to come out of COVID.

— 24, UK

My husband and I had bought a bigger bed and needed bigger pillows. We each bought what we thought would be good pillows for us but mine was terrible to sleep on. About that time I found out he was having an online affair so, in a fit of anger, I switched the pillows when changing the sheets. It was a pleasure to watch him squirm and try to get comfortable on that shit pillow.

He has gone through three different ones and I'm still sleeping on the same good one eight years later. He did confess about the affair, we worked through it and are still together. He never figured out what I did though.

— 62, US

I've always been tall and built on a massive frame, so naturally everyone has always assumed I am much older than I really am. This time was no different.

When I was 16 my friend and I signed up for a poetry club at the local university. After the second meeting, two of the other attendees asked us to join them for drinks afterwards. Being so young and having older, attractive university boys show interest in us . . . we were over the moon!

We spent the night talking about dreams, interests and hobbies. When the boy I was sitting next to asked me if I was a student, I said yes. He informed me he was studying to become a teacher. One thing led to another and we kissed. Lots of kissing, a few hickeys and one perfect hook-up later we parted and said we looked forward to seeing each other the following week at the poetry club.

At school three days later, I walked into my English class and my stomach dropped. My perfect post-poetry hook-up was my substitute teacher for the day.

He realized when I said I was a student, I omitted the fact that I was in fact a high school student.

I have no regrets.

33, Canada

I once hid all of the toilet roll in my office building. My colleague (who I didn't like) used the loo for a number 2 and, when the realization dawned on him, had to yell very loudly, so the whole office could hear, asking if I could get some for him. I told him we had run out so he asked me to get a copy of *The Sun* newspaper that he had been reading at his desk, and he actually wiped his arse with that.

46, UK

I've been married to my husband for seven years. He was a large fat man when we met ten years ago. We could only have sex in one position because he was so fat and had a short penis. It was always me on my back with my legs straight up in the air. Even the foreplay was EXACTLY the same each time.

I tried several times to spice things up but he shot me down every time. I tried to build up his confidence, tried diet and exercise with him, etc. I stayed faithful because I took our marriage vows seriously.

Fast forward several years later and he had gastric bypass surgery and lost almost 200lb. Imagine my surprise when I found our credit card bill had charges to an adult affair page and two charges for over $300 to an adult store. I almost called the credit card company to report fraud because he's so vanilla in the bedroom. He has never even bought me a nightgown, much less sex toys.

I texted him about the charges and said I was going to report it. He replied that he'd made the charges and it was supposed to be a "surprise" for me. Oh, I was surprised alright because this wasn't like him.

When a week went by and nothing showed up at my house, I started thinking he'd ordered something that was really freaky. I wanted to be prepared for my "surprise" and not look shocked or disappointed, so I looked at his emails to see if there was a receipt of what he ordered. There was a message saying that his package had been delivered, but I knew we hadn't got anything. I saw that the order included a $100+ vibrator, nipple clamps, a huge butt plug, lubes and cleaners, so imagine my surprise when I saw that it had been delivered to a woman I'd never heard of.

I checked his Facebook for the name and there she was, and ALL of their messages. She was an old girlfriend, also married with a family. I collected myself then came up with a plan. I immediately copied all of the messages and vulgar pictures.

I'm still working on what my revenge will be . . .

46, US

I was 16 and head-over-heels in love with my first serious boyfriend. He was on a soccer weekend and I decided to drop by. "He was not in his own tent but I found his beloved sneakers "in front of the tent of another girl. The sounds coming from the tent pushed me over the edge so I threw his sneakers (Nike Air) into the campfire.

Thinking of the popping sounds they made in the fire still makes me smile. When I came home I told my father what I did. He smiled, gave me a big hug and told me how proud he was. "Nobody messes with my baby girl," he said.

— 40, Netherlands—

Several years ago my best friend and her husband were going through a rough time. He wouldn't get a job (she was supporting both of them for the fifth year in a row), his mother was extremely overbearing and he had ZERO sex drive (they hadn't had sex in over a year). She worked very closely with his sister and in a town where his mother was a prominent busybody, so was lamenting the fact that a divorce would mean the end of her career in the town she lived in. I remember getting off the phone with her when, all of a sudden, it flashed through my mind: "Gosh, it would be so much easier for her if he died."

I'm not sure where that thought came from, but not four hours later she called me at work to tell me he'd passed away in his sleep at the age of 32. He was extremely unhealthy and had taken some sedating drugs that caused his sleep apnoea to kill him, but for years I've walked around with the guilt that I wished him ill, and it happened. My friend has since met the love of her life and is happier than I could ever imagine.

— 35, US—

My husband and I used to work together at a retail store. The store was a large chain store and we worked on opposite sides of the store. I kept trying to get him to mess around with me in the family bathroom but he refused.

So one day, after months of flirting, my boss took me up on my fantasy instead, and we slept together in the family bathroom, and in the back storage room, and in the fitting room, and in the managers' offices.

I feel horrible now, and my husband still has no idea.

35, US

I was three months pregnant with our second child, our rainbow baby after having previously suffered a miscarriage, when I found out my partner had been cheating on me, not only throughout the whole pregnancy but also while I had been losing our baby.

He has long, curly hair and this is what ALWAYS got him attention from other women, what they would comment on and what attracted them to him.

So I put two bottles of hair removal cream in his shampoo bottle. It genuinely looked like someone had SHAVED half of his head. He thought he had alopecia.

31, Afghanistan

When my sister had my nephew, her partner changed. He was doing drugs and became very emotionally abusive, as well as doing things like smearing dirty nappies inside my sister's slippers. He even ripped the blinds from his own newborn son's window every time my sister put them up.

She phoned me one day saying her partner had locked her and my nephew in the bedroom, so I drove over to help her. Luckily, by the time I got to the house, she had got out of the room and was standing by the front door holding my nephew. But as soon as her partner saw my car, he pushed them out of the door and slammed it shut. They had no jackets or shoes or anything!

Once I got my sister and nephew to somewhere safe, I phoned social services and the police. I was so worried about what my sister's partner would do next.

This was nearly seven years ago and still, to this day, I will never admit that it was me that rung them. I'm glad I did, as it got my sister and nephew to safety and court orders to protect them both, but I will never tell anyone.

33, UK

New customers at Sainsbury's get £18 off their first shop so I used to set up a new email account every week as a new customer to get the money off. I got caught and am now banned from Sainsbury's.

37, UK

I sometimes call in sick at work and still pretend to go to work, only to go home again when everyone has left just to enjoy a day at home alone with no questions asked. And sometimes when I'm actually sick, I still don't tell my partner about it.

47, Sweden

I was in my teens and had just broken up with my boyfriend. Fast forward a couple of months and we were getting back together but in secret, because my friends now hated him.

I lost my virginity to him and thought we were in love.

After that, I didn't hear from him until two weeks later, and when we went out, he actually introduced me to his new girlfriend by kissing her in my face, and she then proceeded to say, "Oh god, you look so sad, I hope you don't mind I'm dating your ex. I wouldn't want to leave him cause he's cute but I'd do it for the girl code." I said no and secretly vowed to get my revenge.

That same night my ex kissed me in secret and I was shocked but not bothered. Joke's on the girl: after that night I slowly befriended her to the point where I became her confidante and basically got her to break up with him when they were having problems (and continued dating and sleeping with my ex in secret at the same time).

To this day no one knows I was the real cause in them breaking up.

—————————————————————————————— 26, France—

In my first ever job, at the age of 17, I got flirty with the boss. We ended up sleeping together multiple times. His long-term partner was the office manager.

—————————————————————————————————— 29, UK—

My mother-in-law hated that I breastfed my babies. She would always ask me to feed in another room when we were at her house, and even once asked me to go upstairs in my own house while feeding my baby!

As my confidence grew as a mother, I started refusing to hide away but always felt self-conscious. One day I was making a brew for everyone at her house, tired and emotional as many women are when juggling babies and toddlers, and I overheard her apologizing to my brother-in-law for "having to sit through my feeding". Something in me snapped, so I whipped my boob out and squirted some breastmilk into her tea and served it to her with the biggest smile on my face.

She still has no idea but years on, whenever I see her drinking tea, I can't help but smile to myself!

33, UK

My dad had married a cunt of a woman. She was awful, and very mean and nasty to me and my sister. Thanksgiving came and we had to go to their house for dinner. I was sick with bronchitis and didn't want to go but couldn't let my sister go alone.

It was our job to bring the pies. I had ordered a sugar-free strawberry rhubarb pie and an apple pie. The sugar-free pie was for my step-mother and her daughter who were "sensitive" to sugar.

Anyway, we picked up the pies and started to drive the hour to get to their place. My sister was driving and I was dying – coughing and choking and all the things that come with being that sick. I definitely got my revenge, though. I grabbed the sugar-free pie and spat all over it. I spit my lurgy phlegm into the little hole on the top of the pie the whole way there. We arrived and were met with the usual pleasantries and all the bullshit. I then handed her the pie and said "sugar-free just for you" with a big smile on my face.

I was taking to my dad later and he asked what kind of pies we had got. I told him and he said, "Oh, they sound good." I looked him dead in the face and said, "Don't eat the sugar-free pie." He didn't ask any questions and went on about the day.

My step-mother and her daughter both got sick and I still don't feel a bit of regret or guilt about it. My dad got divorced shortly after that.

42, US

I had a bullying female boss and hated her. One evening I went to the gym, sweated mega, and took myself back to the office. I danced with my sweaty socks on her desk.

The next day, as usual, I watched her eat her banana and sarnies off the desk. Aaah – the joy of that moment.

25, UK

I have autism. I work really hard to hide it, particularly at work. I'm social, I'm pleasant, I make eye contact and I'm sympathetic. But the minute I'm by myself I start shaking my hands. The emotional energy it takes to hold everything in is exhausting. I wish it were socially acceptable to show those oddities. Unfortunately in the healthcare field – I'm a nurse – it would be severely frowned upon, even thought that I'm not competent enough to do my job. Yes there are TV shows that are highlighting this issue, but it's hardly made a dent in real life.

Can I just be me and not have to pretend ALL THE FUCKING TIME? Please?

36, US

I worked for a horrible boss who was always picking on me and putting me down in front of my colleagues. She was strangely obsessed with the plant on her desk, so every day when she wasn't around I'd pour my leftover fizzy drink onto it and slowly killed it. (Sorry plant, it wasn't your fault but it was either you or her and I didn't fancy jail.) It drove her crazy wondering why it was dying. Afterwards I found another job away from crazy boss and lived happily ever after.

PS: I planted a tree in the plant's memory because I felt so bad.

44, UK

Someone at work used to steal food. So I prepped both my food and a carton of orange juice with a LOT of laxative. It was awesome – the thief got really bad diarrhoea at work. He never stole food again though.

— 47, Sweden—

My mom had an abusive partner when I was a kid. He was both physically and verbally abusive to her, and he fucked with my mind too. My mom had finally gotten her shit together and decided to leave him, but first she had to get some payback. She made him a fabulous crab dinner, but she boiled and steamed the crab legs in her pee! Yes, that's right. She urinated in a bowl and used it as her liquid ingredient! He ate Every Last Bite.

28, Canada

Me and the office manager were always outwardly friendly, but I had a secret hatred of her – she was just so goddamn patronizing. So I slept with her other half – repeatedly! He goddamn loved it.

Her other half just happened to be the boss too, so bonus treats for me!

29, UK

I was bullied horribly in my first year at secondary school. The girl was five years older than me and made my life hell. Fast forward to the age of 19 and I became a part-time receptionist at a hotel while I was at uni. The hotel hosted weddings every weekend and had viewings for bookings weekly. Well, guess who came to take a look round for a potential wedding venue? Over a period of six months she booked the venue, caterers, florist, band and hair and make-up through us and paid all her deposits. Well, it turns out that karma's a bitch!

I was due to leave in the June to go for my year studying abroad, so I was to hand in my notice in the May, with her wedding in the September. In my last week, I contacted each and every supplier on her behalf and told them unfortunately the wedding was being called off and she was too upset to speak to anyone. I erased the booking on the hotel system on my last day and walked out of the door! I have no idea to this day what happened. I'd like to think that even if it just gave her the tiniest amount of stress for a week or so, it was worth it for the sheer hell she made that year at school for me.

37, UK

I'm a veterinary nurse and a few years ago we had an awful vet working with us, an absolute asshole who treated all us nurses like shit, like we were so beneath him and had no idea . . . He was always right and he never said thank you.

So one day, after all the ops were finished, I was cleaning up after the cat castrates, and then I made everyone a round of teas and coffees and I dipped a pair of freshly removed cat testicles into his tea, swished those babies round nicely and then took him his tea and watched him drink it!

40, UK

I dated a guy who was studying for a long and laborious PhD in geography. I hated geography at school – I wasn't good at it and the teacher I'd had for three years through secondary school was awful.

He didn't have a clue what he was supposed to be teaching us, he looked more like he was about to work on a farm than teach a class, and smelt of whatever he had drunk the previous night and was someone who didn't wash much. As a teen, he definitely put me off of taking geography as a subject as it would have meant a further two years of him teaching me.

Anyway, with my dislike of geography, my boyfriend eventually asked me why I detested the subject so much. I poured out my reasoning and thought no more about it.

A few weeks later, we were meeting his friends in the pub and he said one of his birdwatching pals was coming along. I'd not met him before and was horrified when he said that he was a geography teacher, but he reassured me by saying, "It's okay, I've told him you have issues with geography teachers," and laughed.

And yes, you guessed it. Who walks into the pub but my geography teacher from secondary school! It gets worse. Not only did he remember my name but his opening line was, "So your boyfriend told me what you were saying about your geography teacher. I had you for geography, didn't I?" Mortified doesn't really cover it, and the guy soon became an ex.

48, UK

A few moons ago, when I was in university, I brought a lad back to my room for a bit of a touchy feely (as my mum would say).

We somehow got on to the subject of vibrators and I said, "Yeah, most women have one," so he asked to see mine. So out comes my robo cock and I thought, "Hmm, I'll show him what the fuss is about," so I used it alongside my hands. Let's say he enjoyed it!

The time came for him to go. No numbers were exchanged, we'd just had a little fun.

Anyway a few days later I was feeling horny and went to get my trusty robo cock, only to find it wasn't there. I searched high and low, only to realize the cheeky git had nicked it!

Devastated is an understatement. It may have only been £10 but, oh my, it was my best one.

I snooped on my husband's ex-mistress (later we worked things out), and I still do because I want to see her karma coming. And it has!

I'm not ashamed to say I'm glad she got her life turned upside down like I did. Now she knows what it feels like.

My birthday was in July and one friend was coming to my apartment to celebrate, because of COVID. I ordered a birthday cake over the phone and asked my friend to pick it up. When she arrived, I asked how much I owed her. She realized at that moment that she didn't pay (assuming I had paid over the phone) and that she had stolen the cake! They got most of what I'd asked for wrong so at least we didn't pay for it.

I was 26 and I had a really charming boss (who was only five years older). There was always something between us but we never acted on it. Then one day his new car arrived – a beautiful Audi with tinted windows and leather seats. We went for a ride and ended up having amazing sex on the back seat in the woods. The smell of a new car still brings me back to this moment.

So my husband had been cheating on me and I found out. After a huge argument he admitted to it, then left for work. So I had a fling in our bed and didn't change the sheets. When he got home the next morning, he crawled into bed and went to sleep. Hope he enjoyed what he slept on.

— 39, US —

Two years ago, just before Christmas, I found messages on my fiancé's phone from a girl he had met a few times. Being the crazed hormone-filled woman that I am, I took screenshots of the messages and the girl's details and sent them to myself so I could look at them in more detail and also stalk her on social media.

I, of course, left my partner, but I never actually got to the anger stage much to the disappointment of my mates. However, a friend of mine said something that stuck with me – she said that she would love to shit in a box and send it to him and she heard there's a place you can do that online.

I thought it was hilarious but I wouldn't shit in a box!

Anyway, curiosity got the better of me and I looked online and true enough, there is a website that sends poo to people via Royal Mail. Not human poo, but you can choose from a range of animals.

Remembering the screenshots, I entered the details of the girl he had met and, as it was almost Christmas, you could choose festive wrapping paper, so I arranged for a box of cow shit to arrive at her house by post on Christmas Eve, all wrapped in Christmas paper.

For perspective we were together six years and that night I considered chopping his balls off with a knife, so I think this outcome was a tad better.

— 31, UK —

By day I have a very serious/straightlaced job in finance and at night I write smutty fan fiction (mainly around the pairings of Betty/Jughead from *Riverdale* and Lucas/Peyton from *One Tree Hill*). I find it a great creative outlet, have won online prizes for my stories and no one in my life knows.

47, UK

Sex and Relationships Confessions

Hands up if you skipped straight to this section! Don't worry, I bet you're not the only one.

Sex confessions became very popular on Pyjama Party & Confessions after I shared a few stories on my Instagram about vibrators. I literally had nothing better to talk about one day so I did a whole piece about vibrators, showing off my own private collection and asking people how the hell I should use this massive wand my girlfriends gave me as a gift. The story exploded and I was inundated with messages from women who thanked me for speaking so openly about sexuality and self-pleasure, which are still considered a little taboo.

After that there was no turning back.

I became the "vibrator lady" on the internet, a title I wore proudly, and the sex confessions started rolling in, gradually becoming more and more revealing. We went from people admitting to having sex in public places or being caught by parents or kids, to talking about sex parties, swingers clubs and all sorts of other fantasies. Many straight women have confessed to either having sexual relationships with other women or being curious about it. And some men have confessed to being married to women while they are secretly gay. Most sex stories are funny. Something about things going wrong while being naked makes it comical ... Or is that just me?

Lots of people have been caught in the act or had their toys discovered by others. My favourite story about toys being discovered has to be from the lady who found her mother-in-law's toy stash when she was helping her pack up to move house. Nipple clamps, whip and all ...

There are also a lot of people out there who enjoy a little element of danger in their sex affairs. The idea that they might get caught doing it in a public place is popular, and I have to admit the one and only time I have ever had sex knowing people might be able to see me was indeed very exciting. I was in my early twenties and on a weekend away with my then boyfriend, and one afternoon we decided to have sex on our hotel balcony, which overlooked the hotel lobby. We were both wearing robes so it wasn't as if we were totally naked but I'm pretty sure it was obvious.

There is also a lot of shame when it comes to the sex confessions and stories. Many women admit to not ever experiencing an orgasm and feel real embarrassment when this is more common than you think. Some women have confessed to preferring their sex toys to their partners, and there have been plenty of women confessing to making up excuses to avoid sex altogether.

Sadly, something as natural as sex is often a cause of embarrassment and shame, which is why I love sharing these confessions. Not to cause people embarrassment but rather to lift the veil on the topic. Many aspects of sex, sexuality and even relationships are still labelled as "niche", or even fetish and taboo, when in reality they are not as unusual as you may think. Some confessions are sent in with a disclaimer attached along the lines of "I don't think this is a big deal or that I have something to 'confess' about, but I want this to be shared to help those who are struggling to tell their truth"...

I guess it's only weird when we don't talk about it.

This section is probably the longest and has the widest range of stories, from proper funny and oops moments to heart-breaking relationship reveals. It's not surprising when you think about it: we are social beings and relationships – especially romantic and/ or sexual relationships – play a massive role in our lives.

A guy I hardly knew texted me once, and I kind of liked him so we started to chat regularly. One night we started sexting, with me being really clumsy as I am still a virgin. We met twice and the second time he asked me how I like to pleasure myself. I told him what I like and he asked me if I would like to pleasure myself with him being around. I was curious and agreed to try it. I had one of my best orgasms and he liked to watch me pleasuring myself, so we meet from time to time to do what we love without losing my virginity.

— 19, Afghanistan

The first time I gave my husband head I tried to be a little too keen and gagged. I ended up throwing up all over him and our bed. To this day, every time I go down I say to myself "not too far". It haunts me.

24, Australia

I have been married for 11 years and my husband still thinks we had the most amazing sex on our wedding night. He brags to his mates about the fact I said our wedding night was incredible and we weren't one of those couples who were too drunk to consummate our marriage . . .

I don't have the heart to tell him that he passed out on the bed before I'd even entered the suite and that the receptionist actually helped me out of my dress. I had the most amazing night in the jacuzzi bath but he played no part in that.

36, UK

I was in my early thirties and was watching porn online while my daughter was at school. I happened to click on anal porn – something new as I had watched straight or lesbian porn in the past. It intrigued and excited me so I went to get my toys out and found a 6-inch vibe just to give it a go. Things heated up quickly and I got off rather fast but didn't realize that I had pushed it in my ass but let go of it. After I finished I tried to retrieve it and couldn't get a grip. I started panicking and thinking of all those urban legend stories about people going to emergency with things stuck in very embarrassing places. I rang my best friend and said, "What do I do?" She tried to reassure me and to calm me down, then told me to "Sit on the toilet and relax".

I did just that and, as I'm sitting there still panicking, I couldn't grab it out so I pushed and it came flying out and went straight down into the toilet and down the cistern, disappearing forever.

Weeks later I had to get a sewerage company out to empty the sewerage as it was time, and when they opened the vent and put the hose in I was petrified that a bright blue 6-inch vibrator would be sitting there staring them in the face. I went out as I couldn't stay home and face them if it floated up.

— 48, Australia —

I've had a lover 17 years younger than myself for several years while trucking, but my daughter found a phone text to him and then told my son who confronted me. I promised to leave the lover but I couldn't quite yet. Neither of my kids ever told my husband and, to this day, I've not, nor will I ever.

— 59, Estonia —

I was married for nine years and, after the divorce, when I was ready to sleep with other men, I signed up on tinder. After a few dates I was thinking, "Why do I give it for free when a man will pay for it?" So I became an escort!

I did it for about five months and I must say – best time ever. I made so much money and met some really nice and interesting people. Some of them I am still in contact with as friends.

— 33, Belgium

I met up with an ex and his roommate. They were fit, hot 19-year-olds. We partied hard off spiced rum and had a sexy 3sum for a whole weekend. They gave each other head and then had sex with me.

With this same ex, we slept with his other roommate another time. They tied me up so I couldn't move and tried to DP (double penetrate) me. I miss those times. I am now married to a very vanilla husband.

— 36, Canada

Last year, after watching my marriage (of eight years, together for 13 years) slowly crumble into tolerant living together but barely communicating, I rolled into an affair. "Affair" is an ugly word. We'd known each other from work for almost seven years and were friends who shared a lot. Including having bad marriages. We came to the conclusion that what we wanted was what the other could provide.

His divorce went faster than mine, and although we planned to be together, he lacked the confidence to believe I would choose him after my divorce so, in a drunken state, he cheated on me with another co-worker friend. He knew he'd messed up, and came clean to me.

Right when we should have been picking up the pieces to mend our bond, the lockdown came. Then seven months of not seeing each other, sporadic texts and calls from him stating he still wanted to continue with me.

In those seven months, the woman he'd cheated with claimed him as hers (she lived close by so could travel to him; I was too far away) and he was afraid to be alone and avoided our issues. His ex-wife had a major factor in keeping us apart too.

When we could see each other again, we ended up in bed. He was now "cheating" on the other woman. After making it clear he was staying with her, but for all the wrong reasons, he also said he didn't want to lose me.

At work we are still in home office mode, but the one time we were in the office together, it seemed like old times again – hugging, smiling, talking together.

He doesn't want to break up with her because it would be his third break-up in a little over a year. Not because he loves her so much or because she provides a better future.

I still keep in touch, hoping he'll choose with his heart. I need every bit of control not to rub it in her face that he cheated on her with me.

— 41, Belgium

My boyfriend of four years broke up with me and, as I had to move out of his place, my family came to help me move into my own new place. However, I had forgotten about the huge backpack full of vibrators, sex toys and scandalous lingerie that the two of us had collected over the years. It was stashed away in the bottom of our closet, but my ultra-religious parents thought they'd be useful and pack up my things in the closet. About 15 minutes later, my dad came out into the living room with the most shocked look I'd ever seen on him. I realized, panicked and grabbed the bag, chucking it out of the second storey window.

Whoops. I wish that was it, though, but the bag landed on our elderly neighbour's balcony, which she proceeded to pick up and look through and then leave on the doorstep of our place. To say I'm traumatized is an understatement.

— 23, Netherlands—

I have never been the kind of girl to sleep around, date a bunch of guys, cheat or have sex outside of committed relationships. I am a very conservative person in terms of my body and who I open up to sexually, but once I open up I can be a freak between the sheets. Being almost 30, people are surprised to find out that I have only been with as many guys as you can count on one hand. My recent partner and I have been together for quite some time. We have three beautiful kids. And aside from the odd argument here or there, we've got it pretty good as a couple and a family.

But lately I have been having some pretty seriously erotic dreams about cheating on him – with one of his friends. And I am talking XXX-rated, wake up wet in the drawers kind of dreams. Now every time this friend comes over, I get seriously awkward and flustered around him. I mean he's definitely something to look at – he's also six years younger than me – but I just feel so dirty. I would 100% never cheat, I love my man and am as loyal as they come, but these dreams have got me feeling like a criminal.

— 30, Spain—

I'm at the airport, with only the one cabin case. I'm a nervous flyer so I've got a bit of a sweat on as I go through customs. Everyone in the queue seems to be elderly or certainly older than me, mostly couples. I must have been looking a bit shifty as a guy on the baggage x-ray machine kept looking at me. My bag went through and got taken to a table at the side and I was called over. Oh shit, I knew what was coming: a bag search.

There were a few other people milling about and some couples were in the queue to also have their bags checked. So the guy opened my bag and started taking everything out and checking it. He came to the fancy black box. "What's in here?" he asked me. I stuttered, "A . . . a, er, it's a . . . a 'toy'."

He looked at me confused and opened the box, peered in and looked back at me. "A toy? What sort of toy?"

He tipped the box up and shook it and "Madge the Vag" rather unceremoniously plopped out and landed on the table with a noise that can only be described as a slapped arse and lot of wobbling.

People were staring at this point and my face was bright red. I was mortified. He asked me again what it was and at this point I'd lost all dignity and replied in a loud voice, "It's a big, fake vagina, sir."

You'd think this would be the end of it but no. The guy wanted to check it so, after having a good look at it from every angle, he proceeded to stick his entire hand up it, I presume checking for drugs and not because he just felt like fisting it. "For fuck's sake," I muttered under my breath as the spectators around me gasped.

He eventually stuffed poor Madge back into her box and let me tidy up and proceed on my journey.

I'm happy to say Madge made it stateside.

52, UK

I'm a professional career woman and anyone that knows me would never suspect that we (my husband and I) spend our vacations at swinger resorts and secret swinger parties. Living out our craziest fantasies together has made our marriage so much better!

I felt guilty at first, but also felt freedom like never before (so I decided to go with the freedom – ha). When my kids tell me how lame I am, they have no idea that I've had sex in a pool while my husband and a crowd of people watched, have slept with many island men while on vacation, made out with a bride on her island wedding day, had an orgy on my living room floor, met a football player in his twenties at a coffee store and brought him home that day to my bedroom while my husband watched, and so many more sexy adventures. Before my late thirties I NEVER would have considered any of this. I lived my life for everyone else and had to be the perfect wife, mother and employee.

I'm still all of that, but now I have sexy little secrets with my husband.

———————————————————————— 46, Canada—

Back in my very early twenties, I had a boyfriend who was extremely into sexy undies. Exploring the town centre for an outfit that would blow his socks off, I stumbled into a sexy little boutique that specialized in burlesque-style clothing and lingerie. I was a curvaceous size 10 at that point (but not comfortable in my own skin). I stumbled across a gorgeous black underbust corset with a set of sparkling and flowing titty tassels. Back then my gravity-defying breasts were perky and proud. Excited with my new purchase, I raced home to get set up and to defluff every inch of me. Later that evening I stood at the top of the stairs in my granny-style dressing gown beaming with anticipation at the surprise I knew I had on underneath. As he walked in I clumsily undid my dressing gown to show him a sneak preview of the night's entertainment, and to my delight, he charged up the stairs to unwrap his gift.

However, I had other plans and I ordered him to get into bed. I proceeded to climb up onto the edge of the bed to show him my synchronized titty tassel twirling that I had practised earlier, only to stumble and fall, cracking my head on the bedside table.

The next moments were a blur of shouting and panic, and once I came to, I quickly realized that I was in the back of an ambulance with a blushing paramedic. It was at that point I realized that there I was there in all my glory, titty tassels and all, lying covered in blood from a cut to my head on my way to A&E.

Safe to say that relationship didn't last much longer and to this day I do not like the idea of dressing up for any bedroom activities.

29, Germany

I'm afraid that if I tell him I was assaulted he won't love me the same any more. That he will see my body as broken or used up.

19, Canada

Before meeting my husband, I was a swinger with my ex-fiancé. When my husband initially asked how many partners I'd been with, I told him the truth: I didn't know! He was very accepting and kept asking questions of the lifestyle. I knew he was curious but hesitant. Instead, on his 30th birthday, I gave him his first threesome. To say the least, he was thrilled! I thought that would keep his curiosity at bay but, in fact, it led us to be completely open about everything. We've both given each other permission to "play" alone, but we never have out of mutual respect. Having a threesome made my marriage stronger somehow!

34, Canada

I am married to a man and have two children with him but I so long to be with a woman. Any time we have sex, I imagine this one woman in particular and he has absolutely no idea.

My son is autistic but wasn't diagnosed until he was seven, due to tons of other issues. He has several special needs, so in between doctor appointments, specialists, testing, swimming lessons, soccer games, school and just life in general, my boyfriend and I don't get a lot of "adult time".

One day we were sitting on the couch while my son was playing in his room with a friend, about 10 feet away from where we were sitting. My boyfriend suddenly kissed me (oh my god, was it a steamy kiss) and "ding", I was instantly in the mood! He got up, closed my son's door, using the excuse that we couldn't hear the TV very well, and we had the most passionate sex we had EVER had. Neither of us made much noise, which was hard to do. The kids never knew what happened. By the time they were done playing and came out of the room, I was making dinner.

My boyfriend and I have a child together, who may or may not be a result of that day.

My husband and I used to regularly go to a swingers/BDSM club to enjoy both types of activities. Of course we had many amazing experiences. The funniest by far was on a swingers party night. We ran into my chiropractor from my teen years while I was completely naked and slightly intoxicated. I was completely embarrassed at the time but laughed about it the next day.

I have absolutely no attraction to my husband sexually. I keep looking at him thinking that maybe if he shaves his beard and moustache . . . But then he does and NOTHING. I love him, don't get me wrong, and he's great with the kids. I just don't want to jump his bones.

———————————— 38, Finland———

A few months ago my boyfriend and I had a threesome with a 33-year-old guy.

———————————— 48, Canada———

When I was in my twenties, my husband and I returned to an empty house – we lived at my mom's back then. We fell asleep for a while, and when we woke up we had rather enthusiastic sex. Afterwards we went for a shower but when we came back we saw the door that was connecting the living room and the bedroom was open and realized that all the time we had crazy cowboy sex, my step-dad was in the next room.

———————————— 30, Peru———

Many moons ago I was dating a couple of different guys. I went home with one of them and we had sex. He finished the act on my chest. I wiped up and went home to shower. When I got home the other guy was waiting for me. He didn't give me a chance to shower (he obviously didn't know where I just came from) and I guess he liked the taste of the other guy as he was going to town on my chest with no complaints!

———————————— 48, Canada———

Things were rocky with my then boyfriend and he was being an idiot. He stopped helping around the house, and one day he used my toothbrush. That was the last straw!

I went in the bathroom, locked the door, picked up his toothbrush and cleaned the toilet seat with it, before replacing it in the glass by the sink.

_____ 40, France _____

When I was about 19, I had sex with my boyfriend's brother in the dining room on Christmas Eve, when everyone else was asleep.

43, Denmark

After 20 years of marriage my husband confessed to me that he is bisexual. This was shocking only because he had severely bullied me about discovering my bisexuality in the first year of our marriage after I reluctantly agreed to participate with him in a "Ménage à trois". We were so young and I tried to mimic what he had shown me on videos and I didn't know I would enjoy the simple intimate touch of a woman. It didn't go far because he quickly became upset. He bullied me severely after that.

Our marriage survived but had its troubles over the years. He had other fetishes too and I tried to keep him happy, even stepping out of my comfort zone and going to sex clubs with him. It was exciting but failed to keep him happy.

He recently refused to stop chasing a colleague and he was increasingly abusive to me. We are now going through a stressful divorce.

49, Germany

I don't love my husband. I probably never did.

I had just separated from my first husband because I did not have faith in our future any more. I wanted children, a house with a nice garden and to be financially stable, and none of that seemed possible with him. I did love him, but we were in a long-distance relationship and he didn't seem interested in changing this.

So I had an affair. For two years. Oh the sex was heavenly! My lover was so hot and I felt so desired, I could not get enough of him. And he was such a good friend, too. Then he told me his ex-partner wanted him back, and because I was not free for him, he decided to go back to her.

I was an emotional wreck. I got my doctor to put me on sick leave for two weeks because I could not stop crying. This is when I met my now husband and father of our two children. I was emotionally unstable and feared I would never find a man again so I got divorced from my ex and shortly after married my husband. Looking back, I don't think I loved him then, and I still don't now.

Even though my affair seemed over that time . . . it is not.

— 37, Germany

Since my last relationship ended five years ago (I was with him for six years, engaged actually), I haven't had sex with anyone else. Not because I was in love with him (I wasn't) or because I haven't had the chance. It's my choice. I have had cyber-sex, phone sex, sexting, etc but when it comes to actual sex, I can't do it. I need to really be into the guy and I haven't found anyone that does that for me.

Somewhere deep down, I can't help feeling that something might be wrong with me. There, I said it!

35, Greece

My now ex-husband and I were going on our first Valentine's Day date. He was flying us to London so I popped a little "surprise" in my bag for later. We were almost late for our flight and didn't have time to check in our bags, but it was fine as we only had hand luggage. All was going to plan until airport security asked, "Did you pack this bag yourself, miss?"

'Yes," I confidently replied. He opened it up, searched around and brandished the "surprise" I had packed! My fluffy handcuffs. "You can't take these onboard," he said for everyone to hear.

— 37, UK

I was born in Ireland, a good Catholic girl who ended up marrying a Jewish man and converting. Religion never played a big role for me, but it was important to him so we kept a Jewish house. We did not eat pork, kept the Jewish holidays, etc. HOWEVER, when we would visit my parents in the summer, who lived in a small village in a remote area of Ireland, it was hard to get beef products at the time. Most products were made out of pork. So what I would do is buy the pork products (sausages, mince, etc), peel the labels off and lie. Yes, I told my Jewish husband and children that they were eating cows for years when in fact they were eating pig.

I would say I'll probably burn in hell for it, if only I believed in it. Luckily I am Jewish so I don't. Sorry, God.

— 68, Ireland

I started crossdressing a few years back. Slowly but surely, I got more and more into it. It's not gender dysphoria as I'm happy living life as a man but the feminine alter ego is a safe space to detach from issues my male self has, such as depression, etc. I find it a nourishing space for the sensitivity I naturally have as a person.

When I started, I judged myself so much, despite how much it gave me in a positive sense. I think the weight of societal norms weighed down on me initially, and also it was at the time where I had gone through 12 to 18 months of not wanting to live every single night because of severe trauma in my life just prior to starting crossdressing.

Through research and making connections with compassionate mental health experts, both online and in real life, I have come to a much more nuanced view. I've learned everyone who dresses has their own specific needs to do so, as do I, and even though I'm married and it was extremely tough at the start, I wouldn't change the journey.

To anyone going through something similar, I would suggest that more important than just talking is finding someone who is a natural empath and is capable of effectively listening and who will not judge.

The more I have found others willing to sit with me in my darkness, the more I know I can be myself around them in a way that's safe for me.

I hope this may help someone if they are in a similar situation.

35, Ireland

When we were younger and freshly married, my husband and I had a foursome out of pure curiosity. Not long afterwards, we found out I was pregnant and were so scared that maybe it was from the foursome, even though we had used protection! This was debunked by the doctor when we found out how far along I was, but for a few weeks we had to go through all of the what ifs . . . What if this baby is from another man? Do we tell anyone? Do we raise the baby as our own and not say a word? Do we tell him? All we knew for sure was that we may have REALLY fucked up!

32, Bolivia

I've been so hectic with everything that's been going on, and taking care of me and mine, that I haven't had any intimate relationship for over a year now. I don't even have time or privacy enough to push my own BUTTON.

I've been married for 11 years and am 100% bisexual. I believe my wife knows that I am attracted to guys. I know that she knows, and she knows that I know that she knows, but we stay together. Why? Because we've a 16-year-old daughter, a mortgage, a car and a large family network. And when you decide, right, I'm going to blow the whistle on this, everything else goes to shit. It's a very expensive game of Jenga which I'm in control of right now. Do I want to be intimate with guys? Yes. I also don't want to fuck up what I have though.

I found out that my husband was having an online affair with an old girlfriend. So one night, I sat on his face and faked an orgasm and told him that he made me "squirt" for the first time ever. When in fact I peed in his mouth and he almost choked to death.

He was so proud of himself and apparently too stupid to realize what actually happened.

I was working a senior position in finance, miserable with my home life and fiancé of eight years. I had lost a bit of weight and looked fucking amazing. Suddenly everyone was noticing me . . .

I ended up with my tongue down the throat of someone who worked directly for me, and things got quite heated over the coming weeks. We were sneaking out of the office to go back to mine to fuck over the breakfast bar or grab a cheeky blow job in the car. No one guessed a thing and we carried on as though we were good friends.

Little did he know that I was fucking the management accountant on the other side of the room too. This one was classier – fancy hotels, lovely cocktails and filthy sex . . . with an abundance of new toys!

Then they both decided they were in love with me. It became impossible to keep them away from each other at work and, long story short, everyone found out. My workplace gave me a large sum of money to find a new job.

35, UK

When I was much younger, an ex and my BFF decided to move on together right after our break-up. Living on a military base, the flaunting of said relationship was always in my face. One night, after seeing them in the Enlisted Club (the bar on base), I went out and keyed her car, then tried to slash the tyres with a kitchen knife.

50, US

I have been going through somewhat of a mid-life crisis for three years now and it feels far from over. I recently fucked a 27-year-old surfer. He was very good looking and intelligent. I walked up to him, we started chatting and flirting a bit. Then went for a coffee and then he came to my hotel room. The sex was good but not as good as I get at home. But it was a thrilling experience that helped me feel sexy and alive. I don't regret it.

43, Ireland

A few years ago I went over my husband's credit card records – just randomly, I really had no reason to do it, and I found a charge for a jewellery store which I didn't know about. For two weeks I walked around convinced he was having an affair but didn't know what to do about it. He then presented me with the most fabulous ring he'd bought from said store at which point I realized there was no lover and the ring was actually for me. I never told him about my suspicions.

38, Israel

When I was younger, I had sex outside my mom's house in my boyfriend's car out in the driveway.

29, Afghanistan

One time when I was having sex with my boyfriend at his parents' house, we suddenly heard his dad on the intercom (they had this loudspeaker system in the house his mom used to use to tell everyone when dinner was ready). His dad come on and said, "Can you tell your girlfriend to please keep it down?"

Most mortifying moment of my life EVER. We never had sex in that house again.

39, Israel

I sometimes make my husband pissed off at me so we can have make-up sex. Because make-up sex is always the best.

I also pretend I am asleep so my kids won't bother me when they get up. ADULTING SUCKS.

36, US

When I was in my twenties I went to get a massage. The guy giving me the treatment was so hot – like I've never seen in real life. He was such a beautiful man and I'd never had such a stunning sexy man touch me . . . Anyway, as he was giving me the massage, he reached the point where he was doing my inner thigh and I thought to myself he was rather close to my vagina, and perhaps even TOO CLOSE but I didn't care. Like, if he was ugly I may have reported him but because he was so fucking hot I sort of felt a little turned on. I never told anyone about this because I realize it may have been wrong, but I did enjoy it!

— 39, Canada

I am 37 years old and I just found my first white hair. But not on my head . . .

— 37, Israel

When I was in my early twenties I was single and doing the whole online dating thing. One day a guy got in touch but I was not sure about him. We chatted on the phone and he suggested that, instead of going out on a date and potentially wasting two hours of our lives if there is no spark, we could just meet on the street for a short chat and say goodbye, and then if we fancy each other we can later text or call. I agreed and waited for him to show up at the corner of my street. He drove up in a really nice car but when he stepped out I was disappointed by what he looked like – I hate saying this but he was proper ugly and just not my type at all. We chatted for a few minutes and then he said out of nowhere, "I don't think this is going to work, you're not my type." I was in shock! But obviously I played it cool . . . and never told anyone about it!

— 42, Israel

I was in a friends with benefits relationship for the last two years of high school. Everyone knows it's the time in life when you just want to fuck like rabbits every second of every day. It got to the point where we'd have a quickie in the back of the library or in the middle of class in the bathroom. One time we even managed it in the principal's office. It all came to an end when we were busted behind the sports hall by one of the primary school's gym teachers. I went to a conservative private school with some very powerful people . . .

— 22, Netherlands —

I had split from my husband and he was having the kids one weekend. He came to drop them off and asked to use the bathroom. Off he goes and a short time later, after he's left, I go into the bathroom and realize I'd left a vibrator on the edge of the bath. He has never mentioned it and it still makes me laugh to this day.

32, UK

I have to confess that even with three kids, I still have sex with my boyfriend in his car. It's fun and the kids aren't around.

35, US

When my husband really annoys me, you know to that point you want to divorce him, I use his toothbrush to clean around all the taps. In that passive aggressive way it makes me feel so good!

— 43, New Zealand —

I was coming back from a family overseas trip, and when picking up my bag from the baggage belt (with my kids, hubby and parents that also flew with me), my bag was "buzzing". My vibrator had decided to turn on, I knew its noise!

Everyone asked (besides my hubby) what it was and I had a few glares from people beside me. I said it must have been my electric toothbrush (luckily I had one of those). I managed to quickly find it in my bag and turn it off before heading to customs. I will set it to lock it next time. Embarrassed!

— 42, New Zealand

My hubby grew a beard for Movember but he decided to keep it. He'd never really had much of a beard before; it grew fast and it's very wiry and bushy. I didn't mind it until we were in bed and it came to the Australian kiss (a kiss but down under). It's one of my favourite things during sex but now it's awful. The beard has ruined it! I feel like he is just rubbing the back of a hedgehog on me so I end up either faking it or changing positions.

He knows I hate the beard, but he loves it so I didn't say why I hate it. BUT I had to do something! First, he let me straighten it to see what it looked like, but of course I was just trying get rid of the hedgehog on his face. He didn't like it and I really didn't – the hedgehog was replaced with what felt like sharp dry cactus! He was down there with the cactus beard for literally five seconds, and I just said, "Yeah, I came," to stop the pain.

That night I lay in bed thinking of ideas to get my orgasm back, with him snoring away beside me, then I remembered he is a heavy sleeper . . . So I started to poke his face and nothing; he was still snoring so I got the scissors out and cut bits of his beard off. The next day he asks if his beard looked different, and I said, "No, it looks fine." He then looked at it again and agreed.

So my confession is that when he sleeps, I trim and thin the beard a small bit every night, and even put my hair softening oil on it! it's been two weeks now and he has no idea. He doesn't notice his beard getting smaller/thinner. I think another two weeks of my midnight trimming and I should get my favourite orgasm back!

— 30, Northern Ireland

I don't think that my husband has ever made me orgasm. Sometimes I hate being a parent. Sometimes I hate being a wife. I wish I could go back 20 years and redo my twenties and thirties.

45, US

I am secretly bisexual. I probably always knew I was different in some form, but I really discovered myself in the last five or six years. The trouble is I'm in a serious heterosexual relationship, and have been for the last seven years!

I've been with women before, I only watch lesbian porn, and I think of women when we're having sex. I have a "girl" friend, who I've slept with and love deeply, but am too shit scared to leave my current situation. I'm 45.

Nobody in the whole world knows this about me.

45, Ireland

A few months ago a family member came over to help with some essential needs. Once the task was completed, they requested hand sanitizer, so I grabbed the nearest bottle from my bedroom as this was the closest room. Five minutes later I hear complaints that the sanitizer is not drying and can they please have the bottle. I passed them the bottle and was faced with laughter and questions. It was a bottle of lube!

34, UK

I was 17 and had a 21-year-old boyfriend. He suggested we go over the border to Canada for the weekend, just the two of us. I knew my parents would never let me go for a weekend getaway with my boyfriend (who looked a bit older than 21 – and my father to this day does not believe he was just four years older than me).

I had to come up with a different story so my parents would let me go. So I said that my friend from school was turning 18 and was going to celebrate her birthday in Canada because her parents have a summer house there. When I told my parents, they seemed very sceptical and asked a ton of questions, but said okay after me answering them with whatever I came up with at that moment. It turned out I needed a letter saying that it was okay for me to leave the country without them because I was under 18, and believe it or not they agreed to get me that too – we went to the Post Office and had it notarized. So my weekend getaway happened. We had a very nice time at Niagara Falls but to this day my parents do not know that
I went on a romantic weekend with my then boyfriend.

31, US

I've been too cheap to buy my own trimmer. So when I need to trim my down south region, I secretly snag my husband's beard trimmer, do my thing, then brush the pubes out of it before leaving it just as I found it. Whenever I see him trim his beard I can't help but giggle.

33, France

So this one time me and six other gal pals got extremely drunk and had a good time with a girthy hairbrush that looked and felt very dildo-like (if you know what I mean). By far the wildest thing I have ever done! #goodtimes

31, Portugal

In my single years I made love with my best girlfriend. Now I have a man that I really love, two beautiful demons (kids) . . . and yet I'm still dreaming of doing it again with her. We are still best friends.

33, Slovenia

When I was 17 years old, I had sex with my boyfriend for the first time. We then fell asleep and in the middle of the night I just woke up, opened my eyes and let out the most awful long, loud and really smelly fart. I seriously thought I was at home alone, but then I remembered my boyfriend was sleeping right next to me and I started to laugh out loud, but I also felt really awful for being so gross. He woke up and looked at me and then it hit him. The smell. He almost started to cry.

19, Slovenia

When I was 16 and in my first real sexual relationship, I was obviously still living at home. Me and the boyfriend were getting frisky on the sofa. It then started to escalate and one thing led to another. He was giving me oral on the sofa when the front door opened. No one was meant to be home for a few hours but in strolls my bloody dad!

We both quickly jumped up and sat bolt upright waiting for a smack or a screaming at, but my dad casually looks at me then my boyfriend, then the floor. He walks forward, kicks my underwear at me and goes, "Alright," and walks into the kitchen.

I've never been more embarrassed. We literally grabbed our shit, got dressed and legged it out of the house. I was petrified to come home in case he told my mum. To this day she never knew.

— 28, UK

When I was around 18 and still living at home I had an on-off boyfriend. My parents went away with their friends for a long weekend (Thursday to Monday) so he basically came to stay for the whole weekend. As you can imagine we were "making the most" of the time alone, and everywhere in the house. Come Sunday night and we're getting a little frisky on the sofa when a car pulls up outside. My parents!

In a complete panic we shove on our clothes, however not quick enough, and knowing my parents would go ballistic, he has to get into an under-the-stairs cupboard. I leave him there while chatting to my parents, assuming they'll want to go and unpack and get themselves sorted. But no. They've brought Chinese and want to sit down all together to eat. Long story short – he's in there for a good two and a half hours before they go upstairs and I can finally get him out!

— 25, UK

I had a thing with a guy who was 15 years younger than me. We had a very energetic night and we had sex all over the house while the auntie he lived with was away for the night. I have family where they live and found out that he was actually related to me. He did message me on a few occasions, again wanting a repeat of our wild night, but since finding out this fit young man is related, I won't be hitting him up again.

I came out of a lengthy relationship and ended up getting into a relationship with a couple! Completely crazy and totally not my normal, however we had the best year of our lives. We went to sex clubs, performed bondage on stage in front of crowds, and I have to admit it was the most confident I have ever felt in my body!

Me and my husband like to keep things fun with a few texts and pictures while we're at work. Normally they're nothing too risqué. One day I decided to send one of me practically naked, looking forward to him getting home that evening. I sent it and then went to reply to my father-in-law who had text me just before. When I opened the message I saw me in all my glory staring back at me. I had sent the picture to my father-in-law.

I then had to ring my mother-in-law and ask her to take father-in-law's phone before he checked his messages to delete said picture. Thankfully he didn't see it and everyone had a good chuckle. I don't think I'd have been able to look at him again if he'd opened it.

I was in Year 3 or 4 when I learned what an orgasm was. Only then I didn't know it was an orgasm. On several different occasions I was bored in class and pleasured myself.

One afternoon I went out to Happy Hour with a co-worker to one of the gay bars downtown. Happy Hour turned into an all-evening binge drinkfest. The bar had stripper shot boys that night, and I ended up chatting with one. He asked me out on his next break. We went and had gyros, and I ended up having sex with him in his car (in the parking garage). Afterwards, we went back to the bar so he could finish his next set. It was a wild Tuesday night, back when my blood could be mistaken for gin.

— 36, US—

At our very first sex party we were both so nervous. We had been on the websites for a while and done some video calls but then we found we have a sex club pretty close and booked it. We ended up getting very very drunk before going over as we were both so nervous. So we arrive and this woman (who looked around 60) opened the door and showed us around.

It was not what I was expecting at all. I pictured a high end London club with added extras. I was faced with plastic bedsheets and rotating beds! People started arriving, and we were by far the youngest there (we were in our thirties). We had booked a private room for the evening, and again this resembled a room you would find on a stag or hen do. I said I was not going back down but my husband persuaded me to as we were there for the night. I agreed and we went back down.

We ended up extremely drunk and in a three-way with one of the members of staff. It turned out she was a squirter – a massive squirter. Me and my husband ended up looking like we had been deep sea diving after the event. For the rest of the evening we did manage to have fun – with naked karaoke and attempting to pole dance while totally unable to control my own legs. We finally went to bed around 4am.

The next morning we just wanted to get home. We walked downstairs and there was the squirter from the night before who, without the distraction of alcohol, was pretty much an old age pensioner wanting to swap numbers! I've never made an excuse and left somewhere so quickly.

—— 32, UK——

My fiancé, who I had been with for eleven years, suddenly announced that he didn't want to be with me any more and that he had gotten engaged to someone else ten years younger than me. Apparently he had been dating her for three months while working away from home.

As you can imagine there was anger and emotions going round, but three months later I was over it, though we were still living together due to a problem house situation.

Then one night when he was working late, I brought a new guy I was seeing round and slept with him in my ex's bed. Totally cringe, but we left the place in a state and I took great pleasure in sitting downstairs and hearing my ex come home and find his room abused. (It was our room before he kicked me out and gave me the box room.)

Of course he called me all the names under the sun, but it felt so good to do to him what he had done to me, as on that night I told him I had found out about the four other people he'd been with, two of them in my bed.

I like to call that karma.

—— 32, UK——

I used to work at Blockbuster and maybe it was my hormones from just having a baby, but I used to have this daydream about a colleague and how he would grab me and we would have passionate sex all over the workplace. One day I told my best friend and we talked about telling him . . .

He was shocked and amazed that I was having these daydreams.

———————————————————— 33, UK—

My boyfriend of five years and I owned a house together in Leeds but had been discussing moving as I had a new job in Manchester. He wasn't too keen though. Then I found out he was sleeping with anyone and everyone, including escorts.

I told him we needed a date night, and booked us a fancy restaurant. We ate, drank cocktails and had great sex (just one last time) and he paid for everything. The next morning I got up and said, "Right, I'm off, see you!" He replied, "When are you back?" And so I told him, "I won't be. I've bought a house and I'm moving. The removal men will be here at 12."

I had bought a house behind his back. All the furniture in the house we shared was mine so I moved out, emptied the house and took the dog. Best break-up ever!

33, UK

My other half and I met through a swingers site. Both of us were sexually unsatisfied by our partners and looking for that extra bit we were missing, only to find each other and fall in love. Over five years later we are officially a couple with a baby on the way and couldn't be happier.

However, just as we had left our partners for each other, we went to a new swingers club we hadn't been to before and had been meaning to try. We had the tour and were sat down having a drink when suddenly in walks my 70-year-old next door neighbours! They were clearly regulars as they went round greeting lots of friends. I hid behind my long hair and coat, and waited for them to move away from the only exit as we made a hasty departure.

33, UK

So when I first met my fiancé 12 years ago, he started staying with me at my mum's, but the only room in the house with a lock was the bathroom. One night we were getting down and dirty in there, to the point that my mum's lovely new bathroom towel rail got ripped off the wall. To this this day she thinks my brother did it and we still have arguments about it every year.

30, UK

I was five months pregnant and I caught my then boyfriend cheating. We had just bought some baby monitors and I had set them up to check they worked when I overheard a conversation over the monitor about my ex going over to a girl's house that evening.

While he was in the shower I sprayed his boxers with Deep Heat, sat downstairs and waited for the scream. I laughed so much I almost peed myself.

33, UK

One day my husband was going down on me, but a few moments later I noticed blood on the bed. I asked, "Are you bleeding?" and he responded "No". I checked myself and couldn't see any blood on me, but afterwards I went to the toilet and realized I got my period!

35, UK

When I was 19, me and a close friend were chatting about finding women attractive and I said that I'd probably kissed more women than men but I'd never gone further. So we decided to give it a go . . . I decided I definitely liked dick and she decided both were great. I've always said I'll try anything once.

36, UK

Ever stuck your size 7 feet into size 3 shoes? I've cheated on my husband and I am scared he will find out next time we have sex, if you know what I mean?

39, UK

Between the ages of 15 to 23 I had a close group of girlfriends and we had the best nights out. Plenty of alcohol was had by all and it wasn't unheard of, after many drinks, that we shared a kiss between us girlfriends.

39, UK

I'm aged 40 and I have just bought my first vibrator! My husband doesn't know. We've discussed them before and he's of the opinion that it's just not necessary . . . But let me tell you: YES, THEY ARE, HONEY! I'm not sure I will ever tell him; it'll be my little secret.

40, UK

My husband left me a few years ago. After years of cheating on me, one day he just upped and left. I went a little off the rails then – I was 38 and behaving like a teenager. I went on dates and had sex on the first date. I had a 29-year-old fuck buddy. I partied till 4am in London. The list goes on!

But the best thing I did – that I really can't tell anyone about but I would love to tell my ex – is that I had a fling with his friend. His oh-so-fit friend. And I had the best time with him . . . I don't even feel bad, neither does he. I just wish I could tell my ex.

— 41, UK —

I was 19 when I had my first sexual encounter with another girl. It wasn't anything planned or anything I had really thought about. A group of us girls had gone on a girly holiday and booked a chalet. There was lots of partying and drinking going on.

After one night at the pub, we all got back and headed to our rooms for bed. I can't recall exactly how we started but we were lying on the same bed talking and then started tickling each other. My friend got on top and straddled me, still wrestling about. We were laughing then we stopped and were just looking at each other, face to face. My heart started pounding hard because I thought I knew what was about to happen and suddenly I wanted it to happen too. We started to kiss and it was delicious. I was more turned on than I had ever been in my life. We both were.

We undressed each other rather frantically. I couldn't wait to explore her body and I could tell she was feeling the same. It was so strange stroking another woman's body because it was so soft compared with the men I'd had sex with. As my friend reached down and slid her hand into my underwear, I thought okay, this is really happening. I was really wet down there, like the most ever. It felt amazing because she knew exactly what I wanted. Up to that point in my life, I had been with fairly inexperienced men and for someone to be touching me exactly how I wanted was incredible.

Of course I returned the favour. Things were getting really hot and we were both panting and I could tell we were both so turned on we were close to orgasm. I really wanted to lick her pussy to make her orgasm but I was a bit scared as we had gone so far and I didn't know if she would stop me. I didn't want to stop and I suspected she didn't either. I kissed down her body and then her thighs. She didn't stop me though and I buried my face into her until I made her orgasm. I was almost there myself at this point and she happily returned the favour. It felt amazing and I came almost instantly and hard.

We never talked about it again afterwards or did it again. Although I have had a couple of encounters with different girls over the years, I still fantasize about it now. It's probably the most erotic thing I have experienced and you are the first person I have ever told.

42, UK

So I was 18 and got my first sex toy, and it looked like a lipstick in a beautiful shade of baby pink. I had not used it yet when my mum went into my handbag and found it and was trying to use it as a lipstick, but it was not working. I walked in to see her trying to put it in on. I was trying not to laugh at her when she asked me why it was not working. And I can't lie for shit, but with a straight face I told her it had a wax seal that I needed to remove first.

42, UK

I found out my boyfriend of six months had been cheating for a while, so the next time he got frisky I persuaded him to try this new cream that would make him "bigger". I told him I'd put gloves on to make his experience better. A whole tube of Deep Heat (muscle rub) was swiftly applied.

When he tried to shower it off, it just made it worse. And it was even better that he had no idea I knew. I think the effect lasted a couple of days!

I was in a relationship where he absolutely loved dirty talk, and as I was quite prudish when younger, I had to make up all these amazing things I'd done and stories of "activities" and naughty things in different situations and with numerous people. I tell you, I spent most of our time in bed trying to think of things. I hadn't done any of it, but he didn't need to know that!

I was on a gap year from relationships and I was on various dating sites. One night I agreed to meet up with a guy. He collected me from my place and we went for a drive. One thing led to another and we ended up having sex in the car. He was so worried about "stains", as it turned out to be his mother's car!

That's not the funniest part. When we drove back to mine and were saying goodbye in the car, he asked if he could see me again, to which I replied, "Sorry Hun, but you were a shit shag so I don't think I will want a repeat." Then I hastily got out of the car and went in.

My housemate wet herself with laughter when I told her, but it was even funnier a couple of weeks later when we were on a night out in a club and spotted him, and she shouted out, "Oh look, there's Shit hag," just as the DJ lowered the music to make an announcement. The whole club heard and saw her pointing to this guy saying he was a shit shag.

When I was 17 and living away from home, my then partner cheated on me so I was determined to go out drinking. I met a lad and took him back to my flat. We had our fun and had gone to sleep when my flatmate suddenly woke me up as my "ex" was at the front door with flowers and chocolates.

I ended up hiding the other lad in the wardrobe while my ex came in to apologize. He still doesn't know to this day that I had a bloke hidden in the wardrobe that I'd just had a one-night stand with.

———————————————————————————— 47, UK—

My ex-husband was a lazy git, addicted to video gaming, but he loved frothy coffee . . .

I found that spit makes that bubbly swirl look so satisfying. I also used to clean our cat's litter tray with his toothbrush. There are so many more things I used to do. Dipping his chicken in the cat's litter before cooking was another top tip, to get that perfect crunch. Running his razor along the edge of the toilet bowl to blunt it was one of my absolute faves too! Needless to say, I divorced him.

49, UK

I have a higher sex drive right now, but it's not for my husband. It's not for anybody else, but for my little favourite toy. She is black and white and I call her Betty. She is my clitoris sex toy. You see, I love my husband and I do enjoy having sex with him, but during this quarantine I just want to have an orgasm and then sleep. Sex with him is so much more work (which sounds horrible) but with Betty we have a little play around, a few tease buttons and then multiple orgasms followed by a good night's sleep.

My confession is not only that I'm doing this but I'm doing this without my husband's knowledge. He thinks I'm just really not in the mood and the truth is, I really am, I'm just so drained of trying to get him off and then for him to try to get me off, which takes one million times longer than what Betty does. You see, Betty doesn't need to be told what to do, she just knows. I just tell her which buttons to push and away we go.

We ladies need to be proud of our mamma's baths, alone time and TLC with Bettys worldwide.

27, UK

Every time my fiancé leaves his Facebook open on my phone, I go through and remove a couple of women at a time. I'm going to be his wife. I'm the only woman he needs in his life.

29, UK

This was many years ago before kids and I don't know how the fuck it happened . . .

Me and my then partner were really horny one night. I was coming off my period and I thought brill, I can finally fuck. Leading him on to the couch, I had him where I wanted him. There was no time to waste. We were at it and it felt amazing, really different in a good way. He said I felt tight but I didn't care, it felt good and I wanted him to carry on. Anyway, it came to an end. I happily climaxed and my ex pulled out with friction burn on his penis. Not from the sex, but from the tampon I left in by mistake!

30, UK

I'm working from home, and as my husband is away during the week, it's just me in the day while our young daughter is at school. One day my toy needed charging so, with only me there in the house, I stick it on charge in the hallway and go for a run.

On my way home from said run, I call my mum who advises that my brother (17) has "gone for a poo" at my house (we all have keys to each other's houses). I'm grossed out by this as I am every time he comes to mine after school (with the same agenda each time). Until I return home and realize HE HAD TO WALK PAST MY CHARGING, FLASHING, BRIGHT CORAL SEX TOY on the landing to get to the bathroom!

— 31, UK

When I was about 17 I had been with my boyfriend (now husband) for about two years and he dared me to do a sexy dance for him. I decided baby oil and my "sexiest" underwear would make this sexy dance better. Everything started well and he really enjoyed it, but about halfway through I was so focused on the dance that I misjudged how much oil I was using, lost my grip on him while straddling his legs, fell backwards off the bed, hit the wall, knocked myself out and landed in a heap on the floor.

We've still never to this day experimented with oil again and we don't speak about what happened either.

— 32, UK

I'd been talking to a friend of a friend for a couple of weeks, and I suggested him picking me up and the two of us hanging out. Anyway we didn't get very far and ended up having sex in his little car.

I had a dress on and underneath was wearing my waist clincher, tummy tucker, Bridget Jones knickers! I managed to get them off without him seeing but afterwards, I don't know why, I thought it would be a good idea to put them back on while in his small car! He was wetting himself laughing as I struggled.

32, UK

I did not have an orgasm unless I was on top until I was 35. I am now 35 with four kids.

35, US

I got really drunk about 11 years ago and pulled a gorgeous bloke in the local club. I've never had a one-night stand and this technically wasn't one, but it did include a bit of a hand job and a cheeky finger up the bum (his not mine on his request) behind said club. Something I'd never done before nor since.

Anyway, shortly after (I'm talking a few minutes) I bumped into the bloke I'd dated for three years and split up with about two years before. I ended up having a very long snogging session with said ex, who then tells me he has a girlfriend and has just come back from a fancy expensive holiday with her . . .

With this in mind, I decided it would be a really good idea for him to suck my fingers. One finger more than the others, obviously.

35, UK

I've been with my partner for seven years. We've known each other for about 20 years though, as he was friends with my ex-husband. We spent a lot of time hanging out together – myself, my husband and him and his then-girlfriend. We were devastated to realize that we had fallen in love with each other while working together. We fought against it, stopped working together and tried to avoid hanging out with each other. We knew we could never be together, that it was wrong and would cause agony for all involved.

My marriage was falling apart at the time because my husband thought spending time and money with his mates was more important than our marriage and his friend's relationship was a bit of a sham too . . . They'd only been together a few weeks when they discovered she was pregnant, and they'd tried to make it work for the sake of their daughter.

Anyway, while doing our best to avoid each other and get on with our lives, he said he was sure his girlfriend was having an affair. I said it was best not getting involved, but that I knew their daughter knew the PIN for his girlfriend's iPad. She switched it on for him and he discovered secret messages to his girlfriend from none other than . . . my husband! So he kicked her out and I had it out with my husband and left him. We waited a few months before announcing our relationship. To this day, our families and friends, and everyone in our town including our exes, think that we just fell in love helping each other heal through the torment of our mutual separations.

36, UK

Me and my hubby, who I've been with for 21 years and onto our third child (thanks COVID and gin for that little surprise), had decided to spunk up our sex life and start attending sex clubs. We were having an amazing time enjoying this new lease of life. One night we end up in a couples room at a club with this nice chatty couple. We are getting down to business with them when the man pulled off his towel and strapped on a massive 20-inch purple cock!

I couldn't stop laughing! Me and my hubby ended up leaving them to it.

37, UK

I am living a sort of double life. I live with someone, but I also have my life outside the house. He knows where I work but that is it. He has started to say, "I don't think I know you at all". And it is true. He doesn't. All of my family and friends have him blocked on all social media so as not to let him see anything that I post or I am tagged in. He thinks I go to work and come home and that's how he likes it. What he doesn't know is I go out with friends and family, we eat and drink, and go to bars and restaurants, stay in hotels, go shopping, and all of it. I have also had boyfriends. He has no clue whatsoever.

40, US

When I was 19 I was living in Cornwall with my boyfriend. Sex had become beyond painful so I went to the doctor. While having an internal the doctor was chatting and, just as I was saying that my fella wanted to work with precious stones, he pulled a gold earring from my body.

All I could say was, "Ahh, I wondered where that had gone!" He asked me if I wanted to keep it but I said no.

42, UK

I have a lover. I am married and we have two girls and he has no idea. Our sex life is dead, but neither of us wants to end it because we have a good life together. So I have my lover on the side to give me some thrills and somehow it works.

53, Israel

My partner of five years tried to cheat on me a couple of weeks after I lost my mother. We were due to get married, we had the church booked and we were buying stuff for our wedding. I felt so betrayed by him, so I set him up.

I was using the laptop and found he was on a dating site, claiming to be single. He forgot to erase his search history and a notification popped up for him. I created a fake profile of my own and messaged him. I had a date set up with him after only three days. I got my friend to help me – when he called a spare phone I had, she put on a fake accent and arranged to meet him.

In the days leading up to the date, I texted him boosting his ego. I made the date for a Saturday evening, knowing that he was coming home from work on the Saturday morning, as he worked quite far away.

When he got home he invented some story about having to go out as his mate wanted to see him a good few miles away. I said I didn't mind, even though we had planned an evening out.

I'd agreed for him to meet "me" in a pub not far from where he had come from. I actually sat in the same room as him texting him earlier in the day as the fake woman, and he told me he was out shopping. Anyway he set off on his date, he even texted from our car park telling "me" what car he was driving and that he was on his way.

He got to the pub and of course there was no woman. He texted the spare phone and I told him I was still on the way, just stuck in traffic, and to go in and get a drink and that I wouldn't be long. After a few frantic texts of "Where are you?" I switched the phone off.

About three hours later he came back. It was an awful night, cold and snowing, and he was fuming. He told me his mate had cancelled him and I pretended to be annoyed for him and sympathized.

He went off to bed and I stayed up watching the TV. A little while later I texted him from the spare phone and said, "Sorry, I saw you from a distance and you're too short for me." I don't know how I kept a straight face when I went to bed that night as he had a real thing about his height. The next day he couldn't have been any nicer to me, taking me out for lunch.

He went back to work on the Monday and I dumped him a couple of days later while he was away on a shift. To this day he never knew the fake woman was me.

60, UK

It all started after my first baby, who was instant fulfilment in my life. Something felt off with me but I could not put my finger on it. Months went by and I made a friend, a friend I got very close to and we became best friends. And I realized I had more feelings than just that. Then it hit me, "I'm gay." No wonder I never enjoyed sex with my husband.

Months went by of trying to bury those feelings. That doesn't work very well when you are married to a man full of testosterone and all he wants is sex. I knew we both wanted more kids, so I secretly bought an ovulation kit. If I'm having sex with a man, I'm going to need to benefit from this somehow and that was a baby for me. One ovulation test and one sexual encounter later, I was pregnant and then had another baby. And I am still as gay as fuck.

25, US

I've only had one sexual partner and I am married to him (love him dearly) and have recently come out as demi-sexual (a form of asexual). I never had the urge for sex with long-term boyfriends before I met my husband, and now I have a high sex drive for only him.

26, US

I **have to confess** that I have NEVER owned ANY type of sex toy or dildo of any kind, nor have I ever used one or had someone else use one on me. I have not had any sexual contact of any kind in over SEVEN YEARS! But even though I have not had sex or anything at all in those years, I have not once even thought about going and buying something to pleasure myself sexually. Is that weird?

37, Canada

I met my husband for the first time at a kids' pizza arcade, at his little brother's birthday. I was friends with his mom but had never met him in person. At the time I was dating another guy, but when I was introduced to my now husband, I felt a very strong connection and knew the feelings were mutual. After the party I did everything I could for the next few weeks to get the guy I was seeing to lose interest. Finally I just sent him random messages that I pretended to send by accident. He finally got all angry and told me it was over. I was so happy, but I acted hurt and I told my soon-to-be mother-in-law I was unhappy and needed a night out. She threw a party and guess who showed up, and asked me out? Sometimes I feel bad for how I ended things, but it was never serious like the feelings I have for my husband. We have been together ever since.

33, US

Sometimes I pretend I'm on my period for a few days longer when I don't want to have sex.

36, US

I was a late bloomer sexually – always a bit nerdy, somewhat awkward and with very little physical confidence. I attended a parochial school and the lack of sex ed and the plethora of sex-laden guilt (both physical and metaphorical) certainly affected my psyche. Until the age of 35 I had never even masturbated. Never. My husband still doesn't believe this, but it's true. I had so many issues that even pleasuring myself seemed wrong. I always needed for it to be given to me or to deserve it being given from someone else. Holy shit.

My sex life with my husband started out strong, has ebbed and flowed thanks to two children, severe post-partum depression and compounded guilt with a side of physical self-loathing up until a year ago, when I finally decided to get my life together and find happiness. Needless to say, I have found my new groove and want to really get my groove on alone and with my hubby. There's an even bigger problem now, though. I'm starting to need to use toys or my own hands to reach climax, and my husband's performance needs a little "extra" support these days. I'm in my sexual prime, but I'm now worried that I'm going to be stuck having mediocre sex with my partner to then either be left unsatisfied or have to sneak off to take care of myself for the rest of my life.

— 36, US —

I hate having my hubby at home all the time. Now he wants us to work together in a business. No! I need him to go out to work somewhere else for at least eight hours a day. He is like another kid and I already have two. I need my alone time.

33, Australia

So I was dating this super-hot guy. Tall, blonde, buff, with beautiful blue eyes. He had "the V"!

So he calls one night and wants to know if I want to come over and watch the game. I was like – sure! I'm game!

When I arrived he was making homemade salsa. He had blended the tomatoes and sliced and chopped the JALAPEÑOS. He cleaned up and we sat down to "watch the game". One thing leads to another and we're messing around on the couch, kind of just making out. He picks me up and carries me to his bedroom! Hot, sexy, passionate stuff is going on, then he's being a "gentleman" and doing a little foreplay. He's pleasuring me with his fingers and all of a sudden MY VAG IS ON FIRE! It's burning like crazy and I stop him. I'm so embarrassed I jump up, get dressed and I'm rushing out the door. He chases after me asking what's wrong.

37, US

The epitome of 2020 blunder. Honestly, in what other year would this have happened? My husband and me were getting it on and he reached for the lube. But it wasn't. It was HAND SANITIZER! It was ok for two seconds, then incredible burning. I bolted for the shower to find a little relief. Absolutely horrible!

38, US

I had just moved into my boyfriend's parents' place and my boyfriend and I were spicing up our love life. So we went to the adult bookstore and picked up this really cool purple vibrator that lit up and some strawberry edible lube stuff.

One night we felt like trying my new toy out, and in the middle of it my boyfriend pulled the toy out of my vagina and got a panicked look on his face. I asked him what was wrong and he showed me the toy. It was missing the top piece that covered the light part.

I'm freaking out on my back trying to dig this damn piece out of my vagina and my boyfriend also jumped in to help me. Needless to say, we threw it away.

A few months later we were in the bedroom watching a movie and his mom came into our room, saw that strawberry lube and asked what it was for. My boyfriend told her that it was special lip stuff because I had really bad chapped lips. So what does she do but opens it up and puts it on her lips. I could only watch in horror. When we finally moved out of his parents' place, his mom handed us our coffee pot box (this was our hiding spot for our sex toys and lube when not in use). She said, "You don't want to forget your toys!" I turned so fucking red. I could never look at her the same after this.

— 38, US

I have been married for 21 years and have two biological children and three adopted children, ranging from 4 to 16 years old. I also have anxiety, so there may be times that I do not feel like getting jiggy with it or being touched, and I will masturbate before sex because it's less effort than letting him do the work, and I can still have an orgasm. My husband has no idea, and he thinks he has made my world rock, not knowing that I have already done the deed for myself. I do not mind letting him think he is amazing, I just don't have the energy.

— 41, US

My husband watches porn videos in the car and he thinks I don't know.

— 31, Romania

As a married woman with adult children at home, there's no time or place to have sex. So we improvise with a seedy motel, two keys, and act like we met randomly.

I've been married for 24 years and am a mom of four. I was married at 20 and had my first child at 21. I have no interest in cheating on my husband, but the only porn I get off to is girl on girl porn, and never with my husband present, only with myself. I've only had one experience in high school, which was a disaster because I was uncomfortable going down on her, and vice versa. I don't consider myself bisexual, but in the past I have found women to be attractive and have fantasized about them.

When I was married to my kid's father, I lied to him by telling him I was going to night classes when the truth is, I was meeting up with his younger married brother at the lake under a private bridge to have wild, passionate sex. What made it even more wrong was the fact that my husband at that time and his brother looked exactly alike, but the younger brother just knew how to hit all the right spots.

I've been in many relationships and had my "ho phase", and now I'm settled down with my husband of a year. I have never had an orgasm. Ever.

I went to a swingers party that had an element of BDSM. They have a room with all sorts of fun things, and one of the main focal points was a spanking bench. It is very medieval-looking. You lie on your stomach with your knees bent (there is a place to put your knees). You are restrained by your wrists, ankle, and head. Once you're comfortable, the fun begins. This night I had two people using a flogger and whip on me. They took turns and it was great! The endorphins kick in and you get this unbelievable high.

Suddenly, and without knowing it, I had a cane used on me. Yes, that kind of cane they use for punishment. It was too much and I used my safe word. I was removed from the restraints and a lovely gentleman was there to give me aftercare hugs and make sure I was okay. I was feeling marvellous. Then someone asked him why he was bleeding. The blood wasn't his, it was mine! When I was hit with the cane, I must have jerked my hands so hard I cut my pinkie finger on either the wood or the metal restraint. I didn't feel it.

Thankfully the hostess is an emergency medical technician (EMT) and she got to work to get me cleaned up, but after almost two hours and putting super glue on the wound, elevating my hand over my head, ice packs – you name it, she tried it – the bleeding was still very bad. To the emergency room we went. Try explaining that to the nurses and doctor! I ended up with six stitches at the very tip of my little finger. I had to come up with an elaborate story to tell my family and vanilla friends.

45, US

I cheated on my ex-husband. He cheated on me too, but I did it first. Yet I cited his cheating as one of the reasons I left him. He still has no idea.

48, US

When my husband really really pisses me off, I will use his toothbrush to clean the toilet.

51, US

When I was 14 years old I met the love of my life, but we were just dumb kids and it didn't work out. There was a lot of back and forth about wanting to be together, but then he moved out of state and we stopped speaking.

Six years later we found each other again, both married, unhappy, and faking our way through life. We spent a couple of months reconnecting on phone and text. His wife was pregnant with their first daughter at the time, but that didn't stop all the same feelings from flooding back; we felt like teenagers again.

So as teenagers do, we had sex. And wouldn't you know it, from just one time I got pregnant. All we ever talked about when we were kids was having a family one day, but we decided to stay put so as not to hurt our spouses. I allowed my husband to believe the baby was his; he still doesn't know the truth and I hope he never does. Now we're getting divorced and I will still not ever be with the other guy. Crazy how life goes.

29, US

When I was pregnant with my eldest, I reconnected with an old friend who was also pregnant and due around the same time. She became my best friend. She was my soulmate, my everything. We raised our daughters together for years as best friends. My marriage sucks ass but having my best friend kept me sane. I helped her move multiple times, I helped raise her kid when she went back to work, and she was my sounding board for all my crises. She was my person, and I was hers. Then one night I got drunk. Stupid drunk. She was my driver and told me that she and her husband had discussed a threesome with me on multiple occasions. Drunk me said that sounds awesome. I started making out with her, then went home and fucked her and her husband.

And nothing was ever the same again. She left her husband. He still tries to connect with me, but she doesn't trust me to be around him but won't see me, so the only way to get our daughters together is to be around him.

I don't regret the sex itself, but I do regret that it trashed my friendship. It wasn't worth it. Meanwhile I'm still in my shitty marriage and my husband doesn't know because I'm too afraid of change to leave him.

— 32, US

My mother-in-law looks very much like my partner. One day I walked into the kitchen and grabbed an arse – and ... erm ... slightly further round – and asked her to "Come here, sexy." It wasn't my other half!

I still feel the need to bleach my hand just at the thought of it.

— 46, UK

Whenever I get pissy or annoyed at my husband, I think about him going down on me. It's not productive, but then whenever I look at his face it has my thighs wrapped around it and he's not talking. Also he's annoyingly good at going down on me so it reminds me of what I would lose if I kept being pissy.

34, US

In my twenties, even though I was a nurse and married, I became a stripper at a club to feel sexy. My husband was into it and he'd watch me in the audience. Because other girls would come up to him, we had to play it off. I hid my ring under a glove. I would go around the room collecting dollars and slip my husband what I made from the stage and around the room. He'd tip the other girls with the cash I'd just collected. In the end I got fired for refusing a lap dance request. I lasted a month or so and only did it on weekends.

— 33, US

Myself and my husband have been married for nearly 10 years and in that time our sex life has gone from 100 to 0. I thought fuck this and started having my own fantasy about sex (in the form of dreams and imagination) with other people, including women, and having amazing orgasms and not feeling guilty for wanting to explore my sexual desires without him.

— 37, US

I once had my first husband and my second husband living in the same house and I was sleeping with the first while the other did not know.

— 42, US

I've been with my husband for 22 years and I haven't had an orgasm without the help of a vibrator for many many years! My husband says I must have hang-ups, whatever that means, and that it's something I have to work through. He's never said that maybe it has to do with him. I mean, doesn't it turn a man on knowing he makes you feel so good that you cum? Why isn't he looking into "How can I make my wife orgasm?" books or something? I've only had clitoral orgasms also. I hear about g-spots and anal and a-spots and everything else, but have never had the pleasure. Is it me? Do I have hang-ups?

The last time we had sex, I felt like I was trying so hard to have one and it was always right there and then it was gone. I give up and tell him he can just go for his. He never says, "But baby, I want you to cum!" He seems to think if I can't orgasm, it's all on me to figure out. It makes me feel like shit! I can orgasm, it's just that most of the time I'm alone when I do.

— 43, US

I have Prosopagnosia (face blindness). I recognize around 10 out of every 100 people by their faces. For the most part I know who people are by their glasses, their mannerisms, the sound of their voice or the 80s hairstyle they'll never change. My big confession is that some of the people I recognize I can't stand, so if I see them when out and about by myself I pretend I don't. They will try to flag me down and I'll rush to my car and later tell my boyfriend how some strange man was chasing after me and claim I didn't hear them say my name, I was so scared by them chasing me. Some days I love my face blindness.

— 50, Canada

I was raped at four years old and then again at six. I knew in my heart it wasn't my fault, but every time I would hear of it happening to somebody else, the shame and feeling dirty would come back. I have never had a boyfriend, partly because I always thought no man would ever love someone who has been broken and used.

Then at 34 I was told I need to learn to forgive the little girl inside of me who was begging for somebody to just love her. So I wrote a letter to my young self and have forgiven myself. I know it is not my fault, it never was and never will be. Every day I wake up and live, it's a big giant FUCK YOU to the monsters who did it to me and that I will no longer be their victim.

I have made it my mission to change things and fight rape culture, to show women that it doesn't matter if you're 4 or 104, if you are covered head to toe or wearing pasties and a G-String, it is not your fault. You did not ask for it to happen, you are so much stronger than what happened. If anybody wants to argue with me, I'll throat punch them. Enough blaming the victims.

38, US

I am a woman in a committed relationship with a man and we have an eight-year-old daughter together. However, I confess that I sometimes find women attractive. I had some discret explorations into sexuality in my "younger years" but things with women never went that far. Now that I'm "older and wiser", and gender and sexuality is now considered fluid by some, I sometimes wonder what my life would be like if I had taken those small relationships further. I've been a huge ally of the LGBTQ community for a long time and now I realize that it's because inside I am not 100% heterosexual and that sexuality truly is a vast spectrum that many of us float on in many directions.

43, US

I lost my virginity in my boyfriend's grandparents' spare bedroom's en-suite.

19, UK

I was 26 before I had my first orgasm. I was sexually assaulted for my entire childhood, so sex was not exactly something I enjoyed. When I met my future husband, he was horrible in bed (although I didn't know that until much later). We were both quite young but he had no trouble finishing off, shall we say. I had been forced to perform oral sex on the teenagers who abused me, and I had nothing but disgusting memories and feelings about it. When my boyfriend asked for a blow, I did it on autopilot and hated every minute of it. (He wanted sex ALL THE TIME – an 18-year-old boy, and I had literally no desire.) It did nothing for me, and he never went out of his way to help me out, so to speak.

I faked orgasms based on what I saw on TV and in porn until I was 26, when I confessed to a friend that I had no idea what the big deal was, and she introduced me to my first "magic bullet". Now, I have to admit that I didn't even know what a clitoris is, and where it was, and what it could do for me. Discovering the pleasure was like heaven. I would pretend to have an orgasm with my then husband (we have since divorced), then when he either fell asleep or left the room (such a romantic), I would pull out my toy and finish (well, start and finish) the job. I got lost in fantasies in my head. Fantasies with me, women, two men, two women, another couple . . . I would "go to sleep" at 9/9:30pm, explaining how tired I was, then run upstairs to play with my toy. Eventually I gathered more of them. And the fantasies, wow.

— 46, US

I've been cheating on my husband for years. I know many people would slut shame me, but it's kind of my way of getting out of the marriage without actually having the balls to get out of it.

It started when a gentleman from a state 1,000 miles away chatted me up on Words with Friends. I flew out to meet him and the rest is history. It didn't last but I was hooked. I started using a cheating site to find men. There are all kinds on there. Not to make women paranoid, but if you're not having sex with your husband he might be looking for a "friend".

— 50, US —

While my son, who is in Catholic school, would be playing sports for school, I'd be sitting with the other moms and dads texting sexy photos and having conversations with our swinging partners, often incredibly raunchy and detailed, setting up dates and dinners for after the games.

49, US

My ex-husband and I wanted to spice up our relationship. He decided to go all out and talked me into going to a swingers party. I'm a pretty introverted person, so the thought terrified me, but I went along with it. The people throwing the party were very nice and said we could come watch, meet everyone and hang out just to see how it was, and only join in if we felt comfortable. When we got there, after he talked me into getting out of the car, we went in and there were literally people having sex all over the place. Tons of orgies!

We went in and sat down and talked to some people (one or two that weren't actively having sex) and just stayed for a few drinks. We never joined in as I didn't feel comfortable.

The next month we received their newsletter and they announced someone had spread herpes around the group. I'm so glad we didn't join in and, needless to say, we never went to a swingers party again!

— 48, Belgium —

After 23 years of marriage, my husband has developed such terrible sleep apnoea and snores so loudly that I've been sleeping in our guest room for nearly a year now. I've tried every ear plug in the world with no success. And the CPAP machine makes him feel claustrophobic. He also moves around to the point of kicking the covers off the bed.

Result? I'm happy, rested and we get along much better. Separate sleeping arrangements can improve and prolong a marriage. And yes, we still have sex! Although having 17- and 20-year-old sons home all day every day during COVID has proven a very efficient mood killer. It's like being teenagers again trying to have sex with your parents in the room next door. Someone, please hurry up with a vaccine!

50, US

My wife fell in love with a co-worker, and one day at work (I am a nurse), I watched her pack her bags on our security camera while I was stuck in a long procedure. I couldn't even call and talk to her about it because I was the last nurse in our department that day. After 16 years I watched her pack up her clothes and other essentials, and I had to act like everything was okay until the end of my shift.

I actually recorded it all on my phone and for a long time I randomly watched my wife leave me from time to time.

54, US

My wife and I have been married for 25 years. Like most married couples, we've had our ups and downs and, over the years and for various reasons, our sex life has become non-existent.

I've been involved in events in the gay community and while I would consider myself straight, I have been curious about men and have wanted to explore certain areas of that curiosity.

A few years ago, we went to Las Vegas for my wife's family reunion. While we had great fun gambling and exploring the city, I was the one person who was up early – usually a couple of hours before everyone else. I would watch the women and men and would fantasize about having an encounter. After a couple of days of that, I went online and began looking through the personals section of a popular website. I figured the best way to get what you want is to ask for it. I was looking to spend an early morning enjoying some mutual manual stimulation. I described myself and what I was interested in doing.

As it turned out, I received a response rather quickly from a nice-looking guy in the next hotel. We set a time in the morning and he gave me his room number.

I awoke the next morning and slipped quietly out of the hotel room and I headed for the neighbouring hotel to meet with my new friend. I spent the rest of the day with a smile on my face. No one asked and I've never told about the encounter.

— 62, US —

Hubby and I are in an open marriage and have recently and quickly fallen for another girl. We were not looking for a relationship situation from our arrangement but are now in this amazing love bubble together and want to keep it quiet until we know where it's taking us. I just want to shout from the rooftops how happy we all are, but will keep it quiet for a few months so we can enjoy without judgement from others.

— 32, Australia —

I found a strange video on my iPad, and I opened it to find my mother pleasuring herself on camera! Worst few seconds of my life ever!

She uses my iTunes account and so do my kids. I had to run around and check everyone's devices and change the settings, then call my mother to scream at her about all the therapy I would now need!

— 42, Australia—

When my husband and I first started dating we were 16 and secretly dating. We'd been messaging online for a while and decided to meet up. We met up in a park and sat together on a bench, kissing and fondling as kids get up to when "dating". I had never seen an actual penis at the time – not even my brother's or dad's. We started walking away from the park and went down an alley when he stopped. "Do you want to give me a hand job?" he asked cheekily. I don't think he actually thought I'd do it. But I put my hand down his pants (we were both virgins) and stroked his penis, and felt it come alive. Well, suffice to say I quickly took my hand out of there, freaked and said no.

I'm still shit at hand jobs!

— 26, UK—

I had an appointment with my gynaecologist yesterday. She asked me to cough when she was doing an internal exam. I coughed, she jumped and when I stood up to get dressed, I noticed her scrub pants were quite wet. Neither of us said anything.

I'm assuming it's part of the job, but a first for me and a reminder to empty the bladder before future appointments.

51, Canada

So I passed my driving test and my pal calls me when I'm in picking up my new licence and asks why I'm picking up my licence? I've already got a licence? No?

I actually didn't have one. I failed my first test 13 years previously but told everyone I had passed! The weight of that had haunted me for 13 long, long years so let the truth set me free!

— 36, Ireland

After only seeing a guy for a while, I went round to stay at his home for the weekend. During the first night, after a lovely Indian meal, things heated up, literally! During anal, he pulls out, and straight away, I smell poop. I can feel poop running down my leg! I had pooped EVERYWHERE!

It was the most horrifying and mortifying moment of my life; at least I know he'll always remember me now.

— 23, UK

I tell everyone that it is my husband who is not ready for kids, when in reality it's me. We've been married for a year, together for six years and the question about kids comes almost every day. I love kids, just not sure I want to be more than the fun travelling aunt, and I'm not sure I'm ready to push a watermelon-sized baby out of my va jay jay!

— 28, Sweden

My husband is not the father of our son.

— 30, Switzerland

I am in total need of a woman in my life! My dad has no idea I'm gay and would be sad or brush it off as if it wasn't real.

One Sunday morning when I was younger, I was trying to entice my partner to come over to see me. I wrote him a very descriptive message of what I was doing and what would happen if he would come keep me company. Unfortunately he did not receive the message, instead my parents did!

I've been with my husband for 20 years and he hasn't given me an orgasm in eight years. I am 39, not dead, so I have a stash of toys. My youngest at eight found my super pink dildo the other day. She turned it on and buzzed it on her nose and asked me if she could play with it.

When my husband left me 12 years ago, I signed up for a few online dating sites. One was international, and I was contacted by an older man from Ireland who was married. We hit it off and began an emotional affair immediately. Six months after meeting online, I flew across the Atlantic to spend a week with him; his wife thought he was on a business trip.

It was the most perfect week of my entire life! The romance, the talking, the laughing, the intimacy, the SEX! Our time together was straight out of a movie. This man and I have continued our long-distance love affair for more than 11 years now, even though we've never been together in person again. I've since remarried; and he's still with his wife. We've supported one another throughout the years with secret messages, texts, phone calls . . . We are each other's lifeline, and will be until the end. We're soulmates who will never be together. I love him with every fibre of my being, and although I'll probably never see him again, he's the love of my life.

50, US

I'm a single mother of two and recently, due to the early stages of menopause, I am suddenly losing interest in men altogether. But the more I don't want any form of penis near me, the more it seems they just pop up in my damned life. Why?

I literally have lost any desire to be held responsible for a relationship, having had a husband and two partners who didn't even know the meaning of love. I think in the process it caused so much damage to my brain it can't recover!

In my previous marriage, I was raped often in my sleep, called humiliating words in front of my kids. He even used my savings without my permission even though he knows it was for the kids' education.

He refuses to let us go, though he remarried three different women, being sexually active whenever. So he left me but refused to divorce me. So cute!

I wanted to try another penis in my life, but it doesn't work and it was time-consuming and a waste of money. So I decided to live a single life and enjoy the rest of my life alone and content and it actually fits me so well.

No man, no stress, no drama and obviously no unwanted sex!

40, Indonesia

My hubby and I were travelling by car across Europe with our two little children. We were driving for hours and both children fell asleep in their car seats. Well, we felt very kinky and I asked if he fancies a quickie? So he pulled the car onto a tiny road next to a corn field, stopped the car and I was quick to get a blanket from the boot. All the action happened in about four minutes.

We now smile every time we see a corn field.

— 40, UK

I wonder if I am a lesbian. I have always been bisexual and I have been open about that. However, I have been married to a man for 20 years and have two beautiful children. I have only felt truly excited about sex with a woman. I enjoy sex with a man after it starts, but the idea of it brings more anxiety than excitement. I love my husband, I am attracted to him and he is great in bed. Maybe in my next life . . .

— 40, US

When I left my terrible abusive marriage, I decided I would help clean the toilet one last time before I left. With his toothbrush.

35, US

I was sat on my bed after a shower and my twin girls come into my bedroom. My rabbit was down the side of my bed and out of sight, or so I thought.

We were just chatting, then suddenly I was being prodded in the back!

Twin 1 said, "Mummy what is that?" I turned around and Twin 2 has my rabbit in her hand. Twin 1 then says, "Is it your pretend pirate sword from when you were a kid?"

My reply was "Yes, I have kept it all these years so please can I have it back. I need to keep it safe." I told my work colleagues and I am now known as Captain Pugwash.

— 47, UK—

When I found out my boyfriend had dumped me to go to America to see the bridesmaid he slept with at his cousin's wedding, I might have peed in his mouthwash . . .

— 51, UK—

I've been separated from my husband for some time and we have two boys – aged four and ten. I'm seeing a cute guy for tea and sex sometimes and we meet when the kids are sleeping. About a month ago, while we were having fun, my younger son hears us and wakes up. The next morning I was in the toilet and my son was in my bed and started to cry and scream, "Mommy, I found Daddy's willy under your pillow. Why is it purple?" Of course he'd found my toy as we were in a hurry the night before, and of course when he meets his dad next, he asked him how is he weeing without his willy.

— 39, UK—

I've had sex with my brother-in-law a few times.

— 51, Netherlands—

When my youngest daughter was four, she was exploring upstairs and came across my vibrator! I thought I had a great hiding place for it but obviously not! She asked what it was so I said it was a neck massager for when I get a sore neck – never in my life had this happened. A few years later I mentioned I had slept funny to a friend outside the school and my daughter announces that I need to use my purple neck massager to make it better! There was a lot of sniggering from the fun mums and judgemental looks from the stick-up-the-arse mums. My response was, "Yes, I think Mummy definitely needs to do THAT tonight," and I walked off.

45, UK

My hubby and I have been married for nearly 20 years.

When we first met we had both been fucked over with previous partners, so we erred on the side of caution for a few months. However, I got bored and curious. We were in town one day and I needed to pee and his apartment was close by. When he offered, "Shall we go to mine?" I thought okay, it would be good to see his place, but I was clear, "Okay, but no sex." We arrived and he lived in a studio, so a teeny tiny place. I went into the loo – a typical bloke/single guy toilet with some impressive toiletries. Then we switched and he went to the loo. While he was doing his business, I thought I had time to have a poke around. I quickly found the kitchen, opened and closed all cupboard doors like a nosy psycho, surveyed the lounge and saw plants, some art, the TV, but no bed. I thought how strange. Then I wandered over to what I thought was another cupboard, opened it to peek inside and a bed fell out of the wall. At that exact moment the toilet flushed and he walked out to find me trying to put the bed back in the wall. I have never lived it down.

45, UK

My hubby was away on a submarine (many years ago now) and I flew out to meet the boat in Bahrain with other wives . . . with a case of goodies (it had been a few months). When I collected my case after the flight, I wondered why my case had a ribbon on it, then I was stopped by customs who took me into a room and confiscated my sex toys! They gave me a piece of paper advising me to collect them when leaving their country as it is filth. So my sex toys were left behind in Bahrain, but the story is now known by many!

— 45, UK

My husband is military, and at the beginning of our relationship he slept at the base. After two weeks of no contact (or sex), we decided that he would sneak me in at the base for hot steamy sex.

We took a shower and he went to his room. I was putting my stuff back in my bag, then followed him to his room. I walked half-naked into his room, with a lot of dirty talk. And yes, I was in the wrong room. His colleague saw my half-naked body, started to laugh and told me I should take the next door.

25, Canada

I have been friends with my best friend for 30 years, and we have always joked around about being together if things didn't work out with our husbands, but what she doesn't know is I have always wanted to be with her. And the funny thing is, it's not a sexual thing. I love her – like she is my soulmate. I just want to be with her and grow old with her and share our lives together, but as more than friends.

— 40, US

Although I was wild in my younger days, my husband is the only man that I have ever climaxed with. I have climaxed with a toy on my own but not anyone else. He doesn't even know this and sometimes I wonder if that's why I love him so much.

35, US

I have had an abortion and have never told my husband. We just had a baby and after four months, I got pregnant again. I could not handle a baby that soon.

44, Sweden

When I was young and newly married to my husband, I fooled around with my cousin's girlfriend on a weekend away. We've never spoken about it since, and she's also now married to my cousin. She's the only girl I've ever had any kind of sexual experience with.

41, US

I had been with my now ex-husband for about 12 years and we were wanting to try out some new things. He was VERY interested in anal, and although I had done it before it was only when I was very intoxicated! So one night we decided we would try it.

We went and got a bottle of vodka, sent the kids to spend the night with friends, and began our evening! It actually went really well and we had amazing sex. But after an amazing orgasm, actually several, I somehow convinced him to let me try a toy on him. I know had he been sober, there is ABSOLUTELY no way he would have agreed. But here we were. He was lying on his back, eyes closed, OBVIOUSLY not ready at all, and I begin. I got about 2 inches "in" and he freaked, clinching his body causing the toy to LITERALLY shoot several feet away from the bed.

———————————————————————————————— 36, Iceland

As a mom and a "wife", the highlights of the day should involve my child and partner. But . . . some days the highlight is when my kid is napping, my partner is at work and I can enjoy a little vibration session alone, have some chocolate chip cookies after and have a nap myself!

———————————————————————————————— 33, Canada

I was making this spicy stew recipe online that called for a bunch of habañeros. I washed my hands after pretty well, but I guess not enough, because later that night when I was giving a guy a hand job, he started making funny noises and yelling, "Oww, oww!" Apparently, his dick was burning!

———————————————————————————————— 42, Scotland

I love the idea of having two men at once, but I'd never actually have the confidence to do it.

25, Portugal

My pre-schoolers have found my vibrators/toys before. We tell them it's a hammer (standard vibrator) and that the other is used to cut the dog's nails (a Lelo Sona – clitoral stimulator). I'm just waiting until they ask me why I have so many pink hammers!

32, Australia

I only bought dildos and other sex toys to try to convince my ex-fiancé that I was still interesting after he left me, to try to win him back. Instead, I discovered I had actual sexuality, that I enjoy solo time and that I actually love my body after years of hating it! I didn't win him back but I've also discovered that's not for me to do. What will be will be.

My husband doesn't know it but I am filing for divorce, and in the meantime I've been having sex with multiple guys every week. When we had sex two days ago, my husband's dick felt so small and flaccid in comparison to what I've been getting. I'm horny all the time now and I'm worried my vibrator is going to break because I use it so much.

In my school days I met a lovely bloke at a party, we got things interesting and took it to the bathroom, as you do. He was gorgeous, funny, interesting – future husband material. Things got busy and we ended up doing the thing. Sadly, gorgeous, funny and interesting didn't continue to the sex bit. I'd had a couple of drinks (make that a lot) and after 15 minutes of pounding, moaning and trying to help things along I said, "Wow, that spider on the ceiling has only got seven legs." It just popped out, I couldn't help it. We abandoned it and never spoke again.

Until 15 years later when he told me it took him five years to try again after that incident. I still feel guilty now. He's still gorgeous, funny and interesting, but I don't fancy trying the other thing again though, just in case . . .

I watched my dog eating her poo the other day and then she came back and started licking my hubby's face. I have never told him that.

———————————————— 21, Germany —

A few years ago, my fiancé and I lived in an apartment building that was right next to the apartment building my mother lived in. One night my fiancé and I were having a sexy night, which included porn playing on both the living room and bedroom TVs, and sex toys spread through both rooms. We needed to take a quick break, so we went out to have a cigarette, and I just threw on some baggy clothes over my lingerie as we went outside. We accidentally locked ourselves out!

We had to go stay on my mom's couch until we could ask the manager to let us in the next morning. But before we woke up, my 10-year-old nephew wanted to be sweet and go open the doors for me so he could surprise us when we woke up. Luckily the TVs had turned themselves off and he didn't see anything!

———————————————— 26, US —

Twenty-five years ago I went on a girly holiday to Kavos in Corfu. Each night we would get glammed up to go to the bars and clubs.

In the apartment next door to us were two girls, maybe a little bit younger than us. We used to say hi and ask about their day, basically just being pleasant to them. They never went out in the evenings and sat on their balcony reading a religious book.

One day we asked them if they would like to come out with us the following evening to truly experience the night life of Kavos.

They said yes, and the next night we started on a few tequila slammers. They had brought their cameras (the old 35mm type that you had to wind on and you didn't know what your picture was like until you had it developed).

Later on in the evening, they were loving being out and experiencing the cheap cocktails. Their cameras were on the table and we were sat near the entrance of the gents toilet. I thought it would be a great idea to teach them about the male sex organs, being as they proudly announced that they were both virginal. Secretly, to each guy who walked past, I asked him would he take the camera into the toilet and take a few pictures of his willy!

So bad, I know! The girls knew nothing about this as they were too busy dancing!

In the early hours of the morning, my friend and I helped them stagger home, with them saying what an amazing time they'd had.

We took them into their apartment and helped them get into bed. I secretly snapped their luggage labels off their cases and we left them to get some sleep.

The next day they were sat outside suffering with a hangover when me and my friend went out for breakfast. In Greece there are always loads of rude postcards, like little stone gods with enormously massive willies, so I bought a couple of cards and wrote: Dear Mum and Dad, having an amazing time in Kavos. Last night we were so drunk we lost our virginity! I took lots of pictures of cocks and actually liked it up my arse too. See you soon love XXX

We posted them to the addresses on the luggage labels.

I still wonder what happened when they had their pictures developed back home, and what the reaction was like when the postcards arrived. I know I thought it was very very funny at the time but as a mum myself now I cannot imagine the shock and horror of reading those postcards. It was so filthy what we wrote, and the photos . . . poor girls, I feel so bad now!

— 49, France —

When I was 20 years old, I found out I was pregnant. The father seemed on board for the first few weeks but then decided he didn't think he was the father (he is) and dumped me.

My friend and I used his toothbrush to clean my toilet and gave it back to him. I never told him and we got back together, married, and divorced after that. I still have never told him and never will.

So I brought this guy home one night and we entered my dark bedroom. I am post-hysterectomy, like years and years. But had some recent occasional bleeding.

Anyway, we get busy, all over the bed, switching positions like a carney running a ride at the fair. Afterwards he notices a dark area on the bed and I'm like, "Oh shit! I'm bleeding again!" We turned on the lights and realized the puppy had shit on my bed! Best part though, we totally missed it. It was in the middle of the bed, and we fucked all the way around it.

My husband and I have had a rocky marriage for 19 years. Over those years I have been severely in love with someone else who I dated before marriage. Recently I asked my husband for a divorce. Me and my ex just get along so much better. He treats me like a queen and always has. My husband treats me more like a nanny and a bank account. I just wish I'd done it sooner.

I'm so ready to begin this new chapter. I needed to say that . . .

I know my husband is cheating on me, but he doesn't know that I am aware. I have known for years after I stumbled upon some messages he sent his lover. I didn't know what to do and was considering confronting him but decided not to. We have a good life together – two kids, nice house, we are good friends and even have a good sex life. I am not sure why he cheats but I don't want to ruin what we have. I made the decision to carry on as if nothing is happening and I am okay with that.

49, Israel

So we were having a steamy sex session in my parents' house and we moved into the bathroom. We were proper going for it . . . I was holding on to the sink and he had my legs around his waist then the sink came off the wall! Water was going everywhere so I freaked out, turned the water off, cleaned up and left the house. The next day mum called me telling me what had happened (she didn't know I had been there). I had to act shocked as I didn't want her to know it was me, and my little sister who still lived at home got the blame. To this day, no one knows it was me.

32, UK

It has been nearly two years – TWO YEARS – since the husband and I have had sex. I don't know how to approach the subject, so I don't.

51, US

A few years back I got pregnant (unwanted). At the time I was sleeping with several guys so I didn't know who was the father.

It didn't matter because I was going to end the pregnancy no matter what, but I wasn't able to tell the father (I would have out of courtesy) because I wasn't sure who it was.

39, Israel

I was with a guy who was into female domination. It wasn't something I had thought about prior to the relationship, but I was very open-minded. VERY OPEN-MINDED.

We talked at length about the different things we would both like to try and were in a very loving and comfortable relationship. As things progressed he became more confident and enjoyed the odd finger up the bum – fast forward to the request of a dildo up there.

Armed with a condom and lube on my favourite sex toy, he bent over and we both started getting into it. It ended when I accidentally caught the button on it mid-thrust and it vibrated, at which he shot across the room.

I've always said being able to have a giggle during sex is a good thing and it shouldn't have to be serious all the time. Well, this wasn't a giggle, this was a cross-your-legs so you don't pee (or fart), crying, belly laugh moment, and definitely killed the mood.

27, UK

Once I was dating this guy I had been mad about forever and we ended up at his place. We had sex for all of 30 seconds when he decides it's best we're friends! Not because he had cum already, I'm sure! I was so fucked off I went to his bathroom and mopped myself up with his face flannel and toothbrush, and proceeded to watch him wash up before we headed back out.

39, UK

Eight years ago I travelled over five and a half hours to see my fiancé and give him an incredible weekend while he was working out of town. When I arrived – surprise – he was sharing a room with two other individuals. No worries, I was still making the best of this. I was all dolled up and we make our way to get some drinks and play some pool.

The night is going amazing, we are feeling our drinks and, shortly after last call, we make our way to the parking lot and to the oversized work van where we continue not being able to keep our hands off each other!

He lay me back on the seat, pulls my pants down and starts to give me the most amazing head ever (he is the best). So I climax, repeatedly, and he doesn't stop. He never stops until I am crawling away. Then I hear, "Baby, you're so wet, I can't wait to feel you," and then he raises his head up to me and – yes, ladies – red everywhere! Nooo!

I cannot even bear to tell him. I quickly grab my shirt to wipe his face, and just say, "Please baby, don't be mad. Just wipe it off, and don't look!"

I'm sure at this point he already knew what was going on without me telling him! I'm crying and he is now panicking, I dig through my purse for wet wipes to allow him to clean up, clean myself up and make our way to the room for proper cleaning, and we never talked about it again!

And yes, I am still with this person and we are on baby #3.

32, US

I don't have a sex toy, and one evening I was really horny and started to play with myself. Then I wanted to make it more fun, so I looked around in my room and picked up my fidget spinner, and that was the best fun I'd had in years.

36, UK

We have three kids, one who is special needs, so alone time doesn't happen often. It had been a week or so since we last got jiggy and we finally got some alone time . . . We headed down to 69, it was our favourite. I usually lie back and enjoy him up top.

Now I'm long-sighted, so close-up things aren't always very clear but I could see "something". I slowed down the head bobbing and tried to focus. Much to my horror I realized what I could see was worms – rather a lot wiggling away.

I gagged and have never moved so fast, in the process kneeing him in the nose and causing a nosebleed. He thought he had hurt me. I couldn't bear to explain for a while, I was mortified. I guess it's the gift of having kids!

Rather than a night of passion, we went on a worm hunt with a torc. The following morning it was Ovex for breakfast. Safe to say, 69 no longer fills me with pleasure and I tend to keep my specs on!

37, UK

I met my sugar daddy while I was in a relationship with another man. He's been married for 30 years with three children and has paid for me to live where I do. He's spent over £1 million and his wife thinks it's for his business.

22, UK

I got pregnant with an unwanted child last January and as abortion is illegal in Malta, I had to fly to the UK to have a termination on Valentine's Day after the abortion pills I had bought online failed. Only my boyfriend of 11 years knows about this.

34, Malta

When I was married my husband and I got into swinging. I was so innocent and naïve and this, as we found out, was more about his enjoyment than mine. Once at a party, he would sometimes forget I was there and would rush off, like a kid in a candy store.

My fun was being a voyeur. So, all alone and nervous, I ventured away from my ex and in the basement I found the dungeon and blackout room. There were lots of hands, fingers and moans. The heat from all the bodies was intense. I could let go without feeling nervous and the anonymity was wonderful.

I found myself with a lovely smelling female; her body scent and perfume together was so pleasing. It was great to have the power to say no to the hands of others as total consent was a must.

Quite a while later I was no longer a swinging virgin and I was shocked that my experience was with a female – she knew what I needed before I even knew.

So a while later, after leaving the dungeon and getting freshened up, I went upstairs to where the food and drink were. While standing quietly in the corner, this very clichéd butch lesbian came over to me and started talking to me, then she whispered, "Did you have fun?" And said she would love my number. The perfume was familiar, and I realized in front of me was my dungeon date. Boy, did I turn red and nearly choked on my drink.

Once the redness on my face passed, we got talking and she was lovely but not my type, but hey I could always use a friend.

As the party drew to a close in the early morning, my partner appeared, demanding to know where I had been. He was quite angry because without me he was limited in his play, as most couples liked a couple exchange. I just laughed because for the first time I was the one having fun on my terms. He then decided that he wanted to leave as his motor had cooled down and the rules said you had to leave with the person you came with. But suddenly my encounter piped up, "Hey Hun, we've not finished tonight. Want to go back to the blackout room?" He replied that that was a great idea and he wanted to join in and watch, but she turned round and said, "Sorry mate, sausage isn't my meat of choice."

I discreetly laughed and it made my night. I told her I was sorry and that I had to leave with him but I'd had fun. We exchanged numbers and she gave me a long kiss goodbye. From the corner of my eye, I could see the shock on my ex's face. It was priceless.

55, UK

My partner is working from home due to COVID and I'm so sick of spending my days off with him in the house, so sometimes I pretend to go to work and instead go to the local library and just sit there reading for a day. It's awesome.

48, Sweden

I met my husband when we were 18 at university and we would spend hours and days in bed having the most amazing sex. I quickly discovered that he loved it when I was loud and called out his name in bed. Seriously, the louder I was, the crazier the sex was. It did get us in a few embarrassing situations though, mainly when we were visiting our home towns during the holidays.

The morning after one boozy night out, my boyfriend said we were alone in the house so we had sex and he encouraged me to scream louder and louder until we collapsed in ecstasy in bed. Five minutes later we heard his 16-year-old brother's bedroom door open, which was the room next door. I was mortified and couldn't look his brother in the eye for months.

21, Spain

When I was 18 and living at home, I had my first long-term relationship. One night there was going to be no one else in the house, which was very rare, so I decided to cook tea and have "Joe" over for a special night. Things were heating up downstairs in the living room and for once we didn't have to move the party upstairs and have non-creaky/silent sex. We were fucking on the couch. It was loud, it was hot!

Then I heard a key go in the front door.

My soul left my body as it's only about five steps from the door into the living room. Luckily, we had a big soft throw to quickly throw over our nakedness and our discarded clothes were covered by this too.

We lay on the couch and, as I was on top, I just lay down flat and snuggled into Joe, as if I was giving him a cuddle.

Unfortunately, my brother had had an argument with his girlfriend and decided to stay in instead.

What he didn't realize as he made himself comfortable on the other couch is that I was trying desperately to slowly make my way off my boyfriend's dick with no sudden movements, while trying to manage general chit-chat and also not sound out of breath.

My brother asked for the remote. I'd managed to shimmy mostly off Joe at this point and so we both fumbled under our sweaty asses for it, and chucked it over. He flicked the channel, and we had to watch the second half of the film Bridesmaids while totally naked and sticking to each other under this stupid blanket, hidden up to our necks (it was mid-summer) until it ended. Finally my brother said goodnight and decided to go upstairs.

I still wonder to this day if he knew what he had walked into and whether he was just totally fucking with us for his own amusement.

26, UK

My other half claims he "doesn't get drunk", so every time he comes home stumbling and making a general nuisance of himself, I rummage through his coat when he falls asleep to see what money he has left from his night out and generally steal about £20, which he presumes he spent on booze and never suspects a thing. It's kind of an inconvenience payment to myself for all his snoring and fidgeting through the night.

— 35, UK

I'm beyond insecure.

— 56, US

I'd organized a camp-out for my netball team at the end of summer and lockdown, for some girl time.

After a fantastic and heavy drinking day full of laughter, confessions and a campfire, a few of us piled in to my friend's camper. One by one the girls left for their own tent, leaving myself and my friend alone.

As we lay together I reached out to touch her. She touched me back and we were soon naked! She let me caress and kiss her and I went down on her until she came. It was amazing!

We are both married to men, with children, and this was our first sexual experience with another woman!

The next morning I had to creep out of her van with the others already awake! They didn't bat an eyelid when I told them I stayed there but they do not know the details!

— 42, UK

I tell my mom everything, literally, but after my divorce I really struggled in many ways and that led me to declare bankruptcy. It's been 12 years and I've still not told my mom. The guilt gets me constantly. I didn't want her to bail me out like she always seems to have to – life kicks my ass, I get on solid ground and usually a medical issue drops me and I have to ask for help.

————————————————————————— 43, US

I took my teenage daughter to the Titanic exhibition and forgot I'd taken a laxative. All of a sudden there was a vile smell and, pretending it was the old couple next to us, I excused myself and went to the bathroom, took off my panties and threw them in the trash bin in the bathroom. I was wearing a long dress so freed my lady parts on the long train ride home.

————————————————————————— 36, Australia

I tricked my partner into a relationship with me. We were in the same circle of friends and I thought he was cute. I started to pursue him with some flirting and asking him to join me on a date. To my dismay he kept turning me down. No matter how hard I tried he just wasn't budging. We went to a show with friends together, and I even got down on my knee and asked him to go on a date with me with the whole room starting to look. He scooped me up and pulled me close and whispered in my ear "FINE!", with teeth gritted and a rumble that sent waves through me.

I knew we were soulmates and I just had to be with him. I didn't give up and one night, after drinking a little too much, I walked over and kissed him on his mouth. We ended up having sex and starting a friends with benefits thing. Well, the whole time we were fucking, I had told him I was on birth control and I wasn't. I hadn't been for three years. We didn't use a condom either.

In the end something happened and we split up, never to see each other again. A week went by and I found out I was pregnant with his kid.

We have been together for four years now and couldn't be happier. We are trying for a boy now (and yes, he knows about it this time).

I have NEVER told a single soul this, not even him. And I plan to take it to my grave.

#sorrynotsorry

I'm 37 and, at the beginning of summer (during lockdown), I slept with my 19-year-old extremely good looking neighbour! The weather had been lovely and he just kept strutting up my drive with his top off.

The trouble is, he's my step-son's friend from school and his parents regularly stop and chat with me and all I can think is "I fucked your son".

I had a threesome with my best friend and some random guy we picked up at a bar. He was an excuse, and as soon as he came, we basically ignored him and moved on to the main course – each other. We are both straight but wanted to try, and it was amazing.

During my pregnancy with my eldest, our first son, my sex drive was out of control. I'm not sure if it was the extra testosterone raging in my body or what, but I could have sex with my husband before he went to work, take care of myself around lunchtime, screw my husband when he got home and dinner was cooking, and still want it before bed. If ever my husband wasn't up for it, I'd just take care of myself.

After my son was born, the hormones did not slow down. When he was about eight months old, we had to move into my in-laws' home, and space was limited, so our son had to share a room with us. A few months later, our sex drive still on high, we were getting all hot and heavy one night. We enjoy the hair pulling, ass smacking and toy fun – a little rough sex is always fun – so he is pulling my hair, grabbing my ass, rubbing my body and all that. At some point I feel a light smacking on my ass. It's not the normal style of my husband, but I don't stop grinding although I'm slightly confused. It happens again, and then I hear it!

Giggles coming from my toddler as HE is smacking my ass while I'm riding his father!

I'm mortified, and wondering if we have scarred our first child for life, and how much his therapy expenses will cost us!

— 37, US —

In my first relationship I faked all my orgasms. The only time I can remember truly getting any pleasure was when I was a little tipsy, and then it lasted for a second. I really wasn't too aware of my body and what I liked.

— 48, Ausytralia —

I once had sex with three different men in one day, and didn't even shower between them. God, I miss my thirties.

— 45, UK —

I can't cum unless I think of my wife with another man. Even when we are intimate, I have to think of her with him in order to stay hard. It used to bother me because I didn't know why. Now that I have accepted it, I feel much better about it. She knows and says it is just who I am.

36, US

We keep a kosher home. Well, my husband does. I did, and then we had kids. I don't have the time to shop that way now, or prepare food, or clean the fucking sink before or after a whole day of work! My husband is never home for dinner during the week anyway, so on most days, I just say fuck it and cook and use whatever utensils I need. I know there are all sorts of fucked up things going on here, but I have to make it work for me. I'm just hanging on.

45, US

I am a happily married woman and proud mother of two boys. We live in a beautiful house in the suburbs, I drive a minivan and do the school run. I volunteer at the school bake and I work part-time at a local travel agency. My life is great. I truly cannot complain – I know how blessed I am. BUT – and here is my confession – I am so bored of it all. I keep wondering if this is it? If there is nothing else out there that can be added to my life to make it even better? And I keep feeling guilty for having these thoughts. I mean, how greedy can I be – right? I already have it all. Why isn't it enough?

Then we decided to get a few wooden pieces of furniture made and I had a recommendation for a carpenter who came round the house to be briefed. The moment I saw him, I just couldn't get enough of him. HOT does not even get close to describing it. So he works on a few things – a table, a shelf. And I keep adding more work for him so he can come back again and again until I literally have no more room in the house and my husband tells me enough with all this furniture. Only I can't get enough of this guy, so I do the only thing I can think of – I start damaging and breaking the stuff we have so that he can come back to fix it. Yep, you heard it – scratching my own tables, breaking legs off chairs, ripping shelves apart, the works . . . My husband thinks this guy is so bad at what he does, poor man. He's actually really good, but I can't help it.

— 35, UK—

When I was little I used to masturbate but didn't know what I was doing. All I knew was that it felt nice (it tickled). When I grew a little older, I did it at a friend's house and her older sister, who clearly knew what I was doing, laughed at me and I felt so ashamed. It took me years to recover from that. I really thought something was wrong with me; I wish more people talked openly about those type of things.

— 45, Sweden—

When I was in my twenties, I was seeing this guy for a few months. It was still at that stage of our relationship where I would pretend to never be hungry and never need to poo.

So one evening he was coming over and I asked if he wanted to get some food in, to which he replied "Maybe later", and I knew there would be a chance he wouldn't want to eat because he wasn't a big eater. So I ordered a pizza and ate the whole tray before he arrived, then threw the box out so that he wouldn't know. Later that evening he asked if we should get food and if I was hungry, so I said I hadn't eaten and that sure, I'd be up for it. We ordered pizza. And I ate it. I never told him.

39, Israel

My partner is religious and has no idea I don't believe in God or religion whatsoever. He is Jewish, and every year during Yom Kippur, which is when Jews fast for 24 hours and refrain from doing things like watching TV, using electricity, eating, drinking, etc, I would hide in our laundry room, smoke cigarettes, eat crisps and drink diet cola without him knowing. For years he had no idea. We are divorced now and I still haven't told him.

71, UK

Dating and sleeping with two different guys at the same time, with no intention of taking it further than just sex with either of them, makes me feel awful and ashamed. I feel slutty and as if I'm doing something horribly wrong. But the sex is just so good. Like mind-blowing good.

23, Netherlands

I remember the first time I discovered vibrators. I was nine, living with my mum who was single at that time, and I used to have this slight OCD about having all the towels lined up. One day I tidied up all the towels in the house, but I noticed one on a top shelf that wasn't supposed to be there. I needed a chair to reach one of its corners, so I pulled at it and two vibrators rolled down straight on my head. I think I stared at them for a good two hours and then tried to put

About five years ago, when my now husband and I still lived with our parents, we made sure to try to hide our sex toys. I thought I'd done a really good job of concealing our riding crop; it was hidden in either a pillowcase or bed sheet at the back of a drawer. That was until I heard my mum and sister muttering to one another and I was summoned upstairs. Upon going into my bedroom, I found my mum holding my riding crop asking what it was for. I told her (without too much detail) and she said she was glad she didn't ask my dad what it was. She'd initially thought it was a golf club! All three of us were wetting ourselves laughing, and the whole time my then boyfriend was sat downstairs. He'd have been mortified if he knew what Mum had found. When I went downstairs he asked what we'd been laughing about and I'm pretty sure I told him Mum had found my vibrator. To this day he still has no idea.

25, UK

Why is it when a woman wants a threesome, she's a slut, slag, whore or it's just plain wrong? Yes, I'm young, but ever since I lost my virginity last year, I've wanted to explore more sexually. Since then I have a partner who is bisexual like myself and we both decided to dive into the world of swinging.

We joined a swinging website and spoke to some really nice people. I feel this is something, like open relationships, that needs to be normalized.

I love the fact there's so many things we as a couple can explore together, with no strings attached. It's very exciting and liberating, and swinging has made me feel so much more comfortable with my sexuality and my body.

26, UK

My partner and me once couldn't find my vibe, so we used a carrot as an alternative. Let's just say it was cold!

28, UK

I've seen all this publicity about sex toys and how good they make you feel. I decided to order myself one to try it out, but I didn't want to spend a lot in case I didn't like them so I ordered a cheap "massage wand" from Amazon (I've upgraded since to a better one).

The package arrived while I was doing the morning school run, so my partner received it and took a peek in the box. He was delighted. When I walked in he was lying on the sofa massaging his SHOULDERS and begged me to massage his back and bring some oil so it would slip better. I couldn't tell him what the wand actually was for, so I proceeded to massage his back. To this day he has no idea what I really use my "magic wand" for and still gets massages with it.

28, UK

A while back I decided to treat my boyfriend to a sexy birthday treat. I had gone all out and bought sexy lingerie and new toys. Earlier in the day I'd felt a bit of discomfort in my minge, but didn't think anything of it because I was so busy getting ready, and a lovely cool shower kind of helped. Little did I know the twinge was going to get a lot worse.

By the evening, while wearing my new sexy gear, my downstairs was starting to get super itchy and hot. I thought it was the new underwear and kept going. The mood pancaked when my boyfriend asked in panic, "What is this white stuff?" There was no recovering from that and we very quickly swapped from sexy night in to watching Netflix. We are still together, but to this day I can't unsee the scene and can't eat cottage cheese. #cottagecheesedick #helloyeastinfectionyoubitch

29, UK

When I first started dating my husband, I created a spoof account of myself to use with his ex-girlfriend to fuck her off. They had been dating for almost a year and she was the one that broke it off, but they were still messaging each other and he sometimes would inform me he was talking to her via text. There were many stories of their love life he'd shared with me, so I thought she was a concern. He would also always refuse to do anything with me if had done it with her – go to a certain pub or restaurant, days out, adventures . . . You name it, if he'd done it with her, he couldn't do it with me. So of course I was worried about them talking. I always thought he was in love with her. And sometimes I still wonder if she was to ask him to get back together would he divorce the ass out of me.

It's ten years on and although I no longer message her (I spent about a year sporadically sending her abusive messages from this fake account), I do still keep an eye on her. She is still with the same guy she left my husband for and now has two kids. I know where she works and most of her colleagues. I am happily married with two children and another on the way, but it's like a guilty pleasure occasionally having a nose about her life. No one, not him and none of my friends, knows I did any of this and still do.

30, UK

I had a threesome for my first time. I went from a virgin to having a 3some.

28, UK

I was dating a guy when I was 18 for about 18 months, and things got serious pretty quick, so I got scared and ran. We arranged a date night and he wanted to pick me up, but I convinced him to meet me there, but instead jumped on a plane to Ireland and ended up living there for six months before coming back.

Later I found out he'd been planning on proposing that night! Thankfully I have never bumped into him again.

32, UK

I pretend I'm asleep so I don't have to have sex when I can't be arsed, then when my partner is asleep, I sit up and turn my programmes on so I have me time.

27, UK

I was working in a school and a new teacher started. We flirted back and forth for a few months and there was obvious chemistry between us. However, as we're both in relationships, it made it a little more complicated. As time went on we ended up working together and obviously one thing led to another. Before we knew it we were fooling around every chance we got.

One half term we decided it would be a good idea to go in and do some "extra work". Luckily nobody other than the caretaker was in that day, and as he went home for lunch, we grabbed our chance to have rough, hot sex on the kitchen counter in the staff room. It was the best sex of my life, knowing anyone could walk in at any point and that this is the room we all sit in for our meetings every morning. After this we got very creative on lots of occasions and managed to conduct sexual activities in the art cupboard, the shower room and even a quick blow job at his desk. Obviously not during school hours. It was the most amazing thrill and nobody ever found out.

32, UK

There was a period of time (almost three years) where I fantasized almost every day about cheating on my husband with other men (some specific, others random). I even dreamt about it countless times and, honestly, those were the best dreams.

24, US

This is horrible and I've never told anybody as I've just been so ashamed (and don't think it's true but it might be). So when my fiancé and I first got together about five years ago, we split for a couple of weeks and I slept with somebody else. We got back together and about a month and a half later I found out I'm pregnant! Ahh, so I honestly believe it is my fiancé's child, but I'm pregnant now with another one. Let's hope and pray that my math was right and our soon-to-be baby looks like our other child!

25, US

I have been married to my husband for five years. We are both still pretty young and we have a beautiful girl together. Well we just found out about five months ago that I am pregnant again! My sex drive has literally gone downhill. I want sex but when he isn't around, so I find myself getting the toys out and finishing myself. Then he gets home and wants some and I'm like – uh, no thanks.

I was once about to have sex with my then husband and was on top of him. When I got up there was a tiny bit of poop on his belly. I had no idea that it had happened, and he was, "Oh my god, what is that?" Yeah – so embarrassing!

My second child may not be my fiancé's. The dates are too close to actually tell, and after two other miscarriages he's so excited and I can't bring myself to tell him this baby may not be his. The other man doesn't want anything to do with this pregnancy regardless of my fiancé's decision.

I can feel myself slipping away further and further every day and becoming resentful of my family for taking over my life completely. Does that make me a bad mom? A bad wife?

I do try to stay positive and hide how I'm feeling from them so they don't think less of me, but I'm now one of those moms who stays in the shower just a little longer so I can cry without anyone knowing. I wish there was something I could do to find myself again, but I don't even know where to start, and Google has been no help with suggestions. For God's sake, I don't even enjoy sex any more. It's like a chore that I just want to be over with.

I would never wish this feeling on anyone but I do kind of hope I'm not alone. I feel so guilty all the time for wanting to get away from it all. I just don't know where to go from here. Should I continue to silently suffer? Is there even another way?

27, US

One night while I was making love to my ex, my daughter (who was only one) walked in on us. My ex fell straight on top of me with the blankets over us.

My daughter asked, "What you doing, Mommy and Daddy?" So we said we were just hugging. She then asked for milk and a hug.

25, US

I puked on my husband the first time I ever gave him head. I was drunk after my 21st birthday, he held my head down a little too long . . . Then I cried and it ruined my mood. I'm still mortified, and now everyone who knows us knows because he can't keep quiet!

26, US

Once when I was pregnant with my first child, my current fiancé decided to get a little bit frisky. We decided we were going to 69. I was about 20 weeks along at the time so it was safe, but not the best idea in the end. Basically, while I was deep throating him from on top, I started to gag. I normally don't gag on it so I just kept going because what he was doing was feeling good. But then I gagged again and it made me pee a little!

Being pregnant seemed normal but I didn't know what to say when he asked what the liquid was. I tried to fake it like I came and squirted more than normal, and blamed the "odd smell" from my being pregnant. To this day I've never told him that I peed in his mouth, but we did not try to 69 while pregnant again. We have been together for 12 years and now have two children. I will take this one to the grave.

27, US

Sometimes I wish I could just run away. I've been married for almost ten years and I have two beautiful boys (aged four and nine) and I love my family. However, I feel as though I've lost myself in taking care of them and in my work, especially during this pandemic.

I work from home, I teach my kids at home, my husband is always home and I sometimes feel like packing a bag and leaving. I don't know what I like any more because I'm always doing things for others, and I don't know how to now get out of this, especially with all the pandemic bullshit because there's nowhere to send them and nowhere for me to get away to breathe.

Not to mention my husband is currently out of work (but still does the minimum he can get away with re the kids and the housework) and I'm the only one bringing in an income, handling bills, handling the kids' schoolwork, and all of my other wifely and mommy duties, which are each their own separate sources of stress.

27, US

My brother walked in on me having sex with his best friend on the living room couch, and while I was giving him oral in the home gym!

20, US

I am heartbroken right now. I have been seeing this guy and things have been amazing, so of course it had to go completely wrong. He just told me he slept with my ex-boyfriend. Yes – ex-boyfriend. Now this ex was my high school sweetheart and I didn't know he even liked men. A lot makes sense now in hindsight. He did this before me and the recent boyfriend were "official".

So I went over to my ex's house while drunk and stole his cat. I haven't told him yet. But he fucked my boyfriend just to be spiteful so I'm a little mad.

The cat is in a much better home. But do I tell him? Or wait until he says something?

31, US

My husband and I have been together 11 years. He went from best sex of my life to HANDS DOWN THE WORST.

32, US

My confession is that I am married (very happily) but do not want to go back to work after quarantining for so long when my state is still having rising COVID numbers. So I told my husband I wanted to find a sugar daddy. I, somehow, found myself a submissive who is willing to give me complete control of his life while still giving me money weekly. Now I have a husband and a submissive sugar daddy who I don't even have to be sexual with in order to get the money! I feel like I hit the jackpot.

32, US

I lost my virginity when I was 23 years old. I wasn't ashamed of it; I just waited for the right person. I never knew what an orgasm was or how to reach it. I just guess I didn't really care that much about sex at the time. So when we finally started having sex he kept asking me if I was enjoying it. I was not. I lied.

Not until after I had my first child (still with the same partner) did I actually figure out how to orgasm. Update: I orgasm now every time we have sex and it's amazing.

— 29, US—

I don't always get off when I have intercourse with my husband so I fake it.

— 28, US—

My husband (of 14 years) and I are in what we now call an "enabling relationship", which basically means we each do whatever we want, with full transparency and communication.

About a year and a half ago, our relationship was in its "swing" mode, meaning we would find a couple we both liked and swap. We found this really awesome couple (A and his wife J) and hung out a lot! Our kids got to know them and their kids, everyone was getting along great, and so it seemed only reasonable to go camping together.

We set up camp beside an amazing lake, did the whole campfire dinner, and put the kids down to sleep. As soon as we made sure everyone was out for the night, we got down to business in our tent . . .

After messing around for some time, A asked if we'd like some tea, and went out to heat up the water, while me, my husband and J kept ourselves busy.

Suddenly we hear a huge whhooosshhhhhh, and a huge light appears in front of the tent.

We call out to A asking if he's okay, and in a trying very hard not to panic voice, he says he may need all our help . . . ASAP!

At this point we're all pretty much butt naked, so all scramble to put something on us, and run outside to find A trying to put out the gas canister that is on fire along with the picnic mat it was sitting on.

Obviously, within seconds the whole campsite was with us, putting out the fire and making sure everything was okay, not noticing in some miraculous way that we were all half-dressed (I think it's possible my husband was wearing my bra and J's shorts) . . .

It took some time to calm ourselves, but we did end up back in the tent finishing our unfinished business.

34, Israel

I am so bored of my sex life (particularly during lockdown when my husband has ridiculous lockdown hair!) that I have downloaded an app on my phone where you decide your own endings to stories with juicy adult content. I will often sneak off to bed for an "early night" so I can read the stories and have some "me time". The problem is when my husband decides he would also like an early night, so instead of my "me time" I have to lie awake in bed with him breathing loudly – or settle for regular sex.

37, UK

Bodily Fluids Confessions

I never thought I'd write a book that had a section starting with the words "Bodily fluids". Yet here I am, about to present to you the top poop confessions (and there were a lot to choose from).

Honestly, who knew that so many people have stories about wetting themselves? My first experience was a time I went to Nando's with my daughter when she was two and potty training, and she ended up peeing everywhere. I was heavily pregnant at the time with twins, so I was stressed and tired and just wanted to eat my chicken and go home. When I realized what had happened, I picked her up, grabbed my bag and walked out of the restaurant. As I left (without paying), I said to the waitress "My daughter just spilt apple juice on the chair", which was obviously a lie but I just needed to get away. I've never told anyone I didn't pay for my meal, which I guess is a confession that should be in a different section of the book, but it was the "bodily fluids" that made me snap that day, so there you go.

Weirdly, despite these being probably the most gross confessions, they actually don't cause much shame at all. We've had people soil themselves in a variety of places and yet, apart from the momentary "mortified" feeling, they pretty much get over it and are quickly able to laugh about it.

The one type of body fluid that seems to cause people a little more shame is periods, and believe me when I say there have been many of those stories too . . . From accidentally shitting themselves during sex to hiding their tampons in different places only to have them found by other family members or household pets.

We've had moms blame their kids for farting (we've all done it) and people peeing in their babies' nappies. I've read it all. Confessions about poop, pee, vomit and farts are always funny. There's an element of wanting to look away because it's so disgusting but at the same time having to keep on reading.

The good news is that we all have the same bodily fluids and, it would seem, we've all had at least one experience which could be listed as proper yucky. My only advice to you is that you do not read this section if you're eating . . .

Sometimes I get a butt itch which I think is pretty normal. My confession is that sometimes, after I give it a good old itch, I smell my fingers. I have no idea why!

37, Denmark

I once let my dog lick my vagina.

48, Finland

I can't believe I'm writing this down . . . I was eight months pregnant with my second child. I'd gone to my husband's place of work and had this sudden urge to poop. So I went into their public restroom and just started and couldn't stop. I was in there for a while, but managed to leave without anyone noticing. I got in my car and started driving home but halfway home I desperately needed to shit again. There was no holding back, so I had to pull over. I had nothing with me. (Now I always carry a bucket in the car for anything that could happen.) I literally had to shit in my underwear standing on a street. I was so embarrassed, I just wanted to get home then so I had to drive with my shitty underwear around my knees and then half pull them back on to get into my house. I think I stood in the shower for hours hoping to erase the memory.

36, Canada

I once shit myself in my bed. On my sheets. Next to my partner. During sex. AND I BLAMED HIM.

I pushed out a perfectly brown curly shit and I blamed him. I told him that I didn't feel any poo coming out which meant it was probably his.

36, Ireland

When I was about eight months pregnant with my first, I woke up one night with really bad pains in my upper stomach under my chest. They were getting worse to the point I thought something might be wrong so I asked my husband to take me to hospital. He often thinks I am overdramatic, so at first he resisted because he didn't think it was anything serious, but I was convinced something was really wrong so off we went.

At the hospital everyone took it very seriously – after all I was heavily pregnant and in a lot of pain. They did blood tests, ultrasounds, checked my blood pressure and urine, the works. Meanwhile, hubby was needed at work so he left for an hour while I waited for the results.

Then, as I waited, I started to fart. At first it was just a few little ones, but then they got bigger and bigger, till eventually I farted the biggest fart I have ever farted. And with every fart that came out, the less pain I was in.

The doctor showed up just before my husband returned and said that she simply couldn't find out what was wrong with me because all the tests came back completely normal. At this point it was clear to me what had caused the pain . . . it was gas. Literally trapped wind. I asked her if that could be it and we both had a laugh about it.

My husband walked in at that exact moment and asked what we were laughing about and also mentioned I looked better and asked if the pain had gone. There was a moment of silence and then I said, "Yes, they gave me some meds and the pain is much better now. They're still not sure what caused it so I should 'rest'." The doctor smiled, said nothing and left the room.

I never told my husband that what really caused the pain was farts. My only regret is that I didn't say I needed to rest for longer . . .

—————————————————————————————— 39, Israel——

When I was pregnant with my second, I was in bed one night when she kicked so hard I actually wet myself. The bed was soaked but our two-year-old was in bed with us at the time too, so I blamed it on him. I've still never told my husband it wasn't our son that caused the soaked bed!

24, UK

We were celebrating my daughter's high school graduation a few years ago. It was a massive event and all the parents from school were there plus family members; even the Mayor was there. We all dressed up for the event and I wore a new completely white jumpsuit I'd bought especially for the occasion.

As my daughter was receiving her graduation certificate I stood up and walked closer to the stage to get a good photo of her. When I returned to my seat my husband whispered in my ear, "Honey, you got your period!" Yes, I had stood in front of the whole school in my white jumpsuit and bloody ass for everyone to see.

The story gets worse.

I somehow managed to make my way to the bathroom and luckily had a spare tampon in my purse. My plan was to clean the jumpsuit so I would be able to enjoy the rest of the day. But, as any woman will know, taking off a jumpsuit to clean it basically means getting totally naked in a public bathroom. So I went into one of the cubicles and did the only thing I could think of which was to take off my jumpsuit and to clean it in the toilet water . . . yes I used the toilet water to clean my blood off the outfit and then proceeded to go back to my seat, jumpsuit on, no knickers until the ceremony finished. It is possibly the most disgusting thing I have ever had to do!

39, Israel

On a cold night, I'd gone "out out" with my best friend of ten years, and her friend who I had only known for days. We made our usual end-of-the-night pit-stop at the mostly empty McDonald's. At this point I had already "broken the seal", so I was running on a bladder that had aged around 80 years due to the alcohol intake (and water in between which never actually helps with keeping you sober).

Walking to the car, the new acquaintance received a booty call and said she only wanted to talk to the guy. As we were already hyped up, my best friend, who was sober as she doesn't drink, said we'd drop her there and wait outside for her to have the chat and then drop her home as planned.

Let's just say, it was clear she wasn't just chatting. At this point I'm in the car with my best friend and I'm absolutely desperate for the loo. She refuses to go back to McDonald's as her friend may come out any minute; I decide to hold. Thirty minutes later and I was absolutely bursting; I had no choice but to squat in the bushes. I found a quiet and secluded spot in the dark, between a wall and a bush. I was wearing a jumpsuit with no bra, so I had to fully remove it and my knickers, holding them in my hand so I didn't wet my own clothes. Mid flow, I see that my surroundings are lit up by some light and, as I lift my head up, I see the acquaintance and her guy.

I am mid flow. I can't stop. And to top it off, I am naked . . . I literally say, "Oh hey, had a nice chat? You must be Josh, nice to meet you," and I suddenly realize I'm urinating in this person's front garden . . . I am still going, fully naked with my clothes in my hand, the girl holding her hands over her face and turning away, while the guy is staring me out with a frown as I'm still going. They turn around to go back in, I quickly clothe myself again and get in the car explaining to my best friend what just happened. She's pissing herself laughing at the wheel as her friend steps back into the car.

25, UK

We were once getting our bathroom refitted by the landlord. He was determined to do it all himself (he was not a plumber and never will be). He turned up unexpectedly while we were out at work one day and removed the toilet completely. I returned from work desperate for the toilet only to discover it missing!

I was desperate and, unfortunately, it was a number two I needed. I waited as long as I could because he kept telling me he was almost done and would be putting the toilet back in ten minutes. I clenched and thought I'll wait it out.

Unfortunately the ten minutes went on and, 30 minutes later, I had to desperately walk past him to get a black bag, and then go into our bedroom (the only other room in the flat) and poop into the black bag using make-up wipes to clean up!

I then had to do a shameful walk past my landlord with the black bin bag now full of my poop to go to the outside bin and dispose of all evidence!

He must have known as I didn't have to ask about the toilet again!

— 25, UK

I had just finished running a half marathon and was walking back to my car when I realized I needed to poo! There were no bathrooms anywhere close to where I was parked. I had to poo in a takeaway coffee cup. I then forgot to take it out when I got home . . . I found it in the car three days later.

— 30, UK

When pregnant with my son, I was well overdue, fat, exhausted and, as it was the middle of August, profusely sweating constantly. I'd had enough and decided to take castor oil to help bring on labour. Well, the labour began before the castor oil had kicked in and as I was pushing my son out, I shat myself. I know I did and my other half knows I did, I could tell with the look on his face.

My son is now nine, and for nine years I've pretended not to know what happened that day. Every now and again, when talking about the kids, I ask my husband what he thought of childbirth and bless him, he's never once told me what he saw. Even when I ask him outright if I shat myself during labour, he will always answer with, "No love, you were amazing."

— 32, UK—

After an emergency C-section with my son, my first child, I was given a lot of drugs that bung you up, mainly morphine. I was discharged from hospital without doing a poo; they never asked and I didn't know it was usually a requirement.

So fast forward to four days of being home post-surgery and I still hadn't done a poo. I was bloated, uncomfortable and in pain, so I sent my husband out for some herbal laxatives. I took one that night, hopeful for a soft stool in the morning. No such joy. Another day of pain ensued. I was scared to eat, and ended up crying on the toilet trying to push one out. It was horrendous.

So that night I took another two herbal laxatives . . .

I put my son down after a 4am feed and decided to be naughty and try having a cigarette to encourage the impending shit to make an appearance.

At this point I should add that I share my front step with my neighbour; he lives in the flat downstairs.

So it's the middle of the night and I'm on my front step smoking, wearing only a nightie. The smoking (and maybe the two herbal laxatives) SUDDENLY kicked in! There was no time to run up the stairs to my flat and sit on the toilet, this poo was coming now. I had no choice but to squat on the grass next to my step and let the poo flow. It was beautifully glorious free-flowing poop! Lit by a full moon! I felt incredible.

Nobody saw me so I thought I'd gotten away with it, I just had to clean up the poo. I got a plastic bag and picked up as much of my shit as I could. I thought I'd done a pretty good job, until the next day.

My neighbour knocked on the door the next morning and told me that there was shit all over our grass, that the foxes were getting more and more tame. He thought they must be eating more human food because their shit looks and smells more human, and that we really needed to do something about it.

I was horrified and just stood nodding at him. I didn't say a word.

————— 33, UK—

On a work Christmas night out I was so drunk that I missed my train home and had to stay on the sofa of a colleague. If throwing up in his kitchen sink wasn't bad enough, I then had to go for a poo during the night. Having IBS means that when I need to go I have very little choice about holding it. Anyway, after I'd done my business I went to wipe myself only to discover there was no toilet tissue. After hunting for a little while in my drunk state, I decided the only thing to do was to take off my sock and use it to wipe my bum. After I'd finished I washed it in the sink and left it to dry. A few hours later I had to endure a three-hour train ride home wearing said sock, which was still wet. I cringe whenever I think about it.

————— 36, UK—

A few years ago now I was walking with my husband to our local Blockbuster video store to return a DVD. I had just eaten a Tuscan bean soup – this is relevant . . .

We were on our way back home and all of a sudden my stomach started to feel a bit odd. I could feel the shit coming and I couldn't stop it. I made my husband stop so I could walk really fast home, but it was too late. I shat myself, but the saving grace was that I was wearing leggings tucked into pixie boots so it just sort of "pooled" at my ankles.

— 40, UK

My now ex sat next to my sister on a flight. She'd just got her period and had gotten some on her overshirt. My ex (who at the time was cheating on me with the married head chorister of a northern cathedral, getting her pregnant while I recovered from an ectopic pregnancy, unknown to me of course) thought it was a chocolate stain, so proceeded to lick his thumb and try to clean the stain for her; she could only look on in horror as he relicked his thumb several times to give the mark a good scrub. Just desserts. Literally.

40, UK

Years ago, when I was very very drunk, I needed the loo after getting into bed, so I got up and walked into the airing cupboard, lifted the lid on the bedding basket (which was around the same height as a toilet), and peed in it just as my partner walked in. I then pretended I hadn't actually peed and had just sat down, and laughed, saying, "Oops, that was lucky!" And quickly went into the bathroom.

41, UK

My husband and I attended a wedding of one of his colleagues. He works in motorsports so there were a few guys at the wedding that love themselves. We were about 15 shots of tequila in and everyone is dancing like nutters and on the speakers starts "Come on, Eileen"...
At the time of this wedding I'd had five children – it's important to know that!

Anyway I'm dancing and jumping and kicking away when, all of a sudden, pee leaks from me and, as I kick, it gets flung into the face of one of the "I love myself" men.

He looks at me and I pretend to have had the same thing happen to me, and look up at the ceiling as if water had dripped on me.

41, UK

I love my father-in-law very much, but as a busy working mum I used to get sick of him frowning when my daughter needed feeding. He had such a Victorian approach to me breastfeeding in front of him (discreetly of course) that one day I took my revenge and used my milk in his tea.

I have since "fessed up", many years later.

43, UK

I was desperate for a wee after a night out and everywhere was closed, so I found a quiet, fairly dark spot down an alley and crouched down with my knickers round my ankles and started to wee.

Suddenly I heard a loud knock and I turned around (still mid-wee) to see a group of faces smiling and waving at me from a pub that was at the side of me! I was mortified. The pub was having a lock-in and I hadn't noticed all the lights on!

49, UK

When I first started my periods aged 11, I was so confused and embarrassed by them that I didn't tell anyone and I used to hide my dirty sanitary products in my jewellery box during the day and sneak them into the bin at night-time. I did this for six months before my step-dad caught me doing it.

———————————————————— 24, UK—

I am heavily pregnant with baby no 2 and I swum lots during both pregnancies. One night I went for my swim, got out the pool DESPERATE for a wee. (I don't do the pool-side toilets where you have to go in barefoot.) I'm trying very quickly to get dressed to use the toilets on the way out of the building. Trying, trying, trying . . . Then, as I get my clothes out of the swim bag (which happens to be the swim bag I also use to take my one-year-old swimming), I find a nappy. Size 5. Yep, you've guessed it. I stand there. Like a massively pregnant whale. And do an endless piss, like a horse piss, into a baby's nappy. And then I am unsure of how to dispose of said nappy, which weighs about 8 fucking stone. So I wrap it in my towel and when I get home, dump it in the outdoor bin so my partner can't see.

When I confessed to my mum later, she half-pissed her pants in the kitchen. Guess I inherited her shit bladder!

———————————————————— 35, UK—

A few years back I had a really bad stomach bug. Unfortunately, on one occasion I didn't quite make it to the downstairs toilet and I shat on the kitchen floor. Not just your average shit, one of the particularly disgusting, stinking variety!

I went to the toilet to finish off what I'd started and when I got back I found my dog sitting where the puddle of shit had previously been, licking her lips! Ewwwww!

To make matters worse, the mother-in-law came round for a cup of tea later that day and invited our dog to sit on her lap, where she proceeded to lick her face!

38, UK

When I was 17, I moved to London to nanny for an Italian family. I had a bedroom and bathroom at the top of the house. I was really nervous when I first moved in – new job, new home, fiery Italians! Anyway, on my first night there I did a huge poo which refused to flush.

I obviously didn't want to bother my new employers with this embarrassing problem so I put my hand in the loo (makes me heave just thinking about it), pulled out this pretty solid and sizeable poo, and wrapped it in toilet roll.

Now, what to do with it? Their garden backed out on to a park so I opened my bedroom window and took aim. Turns out my aim was rubbish and it landed with a splat in their very small patioed back garden.

Next morning my employer went outside for her morning cigarette and walked in said poo . . .

41, UK

I was cleaning around the house with my new cleaning, vibrating brush which cleans all the hard places. I got to the bathroom and was about to use it on the toilet but the power on it ran out! I was gutted so looked around to see what else I could use and there was my husband's electric toothbrush . . .

Perfect! So I cleaned the toilet with it, all round the rim – the lot!

I meant to throw the head of the toothbrush away but got totally distracted by my children (I do have six), so that night I went to bed and, to my horror, I hear my husband brushing his teeth!

That's right, he was basically brushing his teeth with wee and poop!

When I was younger I had argued with my mum and, as a punishment, I had to make lunch for her and my sister. It was a Saturday and I wanted to go out with my friends.

I remember making the ham sandwiches and then spitting in both sandwiches. It wasn't just a little pfft, it was a great big from the back of the throat globule, so big I had to spread it thin over the ham. I then sat and smirked while I watched them eat their lunch, much like how I'm smirking and laughing inside now. Sorry not sorry.

I used to be so ashamed of the discharge from my vagina, then my now husband told me when we first hooked up that my puss tasted amazing. I was always so worried about it, but my husband was like "Gimme that".

In our new house we have three bathrooms. One is outside for garden use and is so gross (the whole house is old and needs a proper do-over). My three-year-old son's bedroom has the tiniest bathroom I've ever seen in my life and we use the space to store nappies and wipes. Our main bathroom is beautiful and big. However, when my husband is home, and during lockdown that was all the time, he takes so long in the bathroom that often I would need to use the toilet too (we don't use the other two at all, ever). Sometimes not only does he take ages, but the smell is potent enough to kill! So since having just had my baby girl in April – well, you know what happens to our bladders – I ended up peeing downstairs in a container! What's worse, the container is the Tommee Tippee flask container used to heat up milk bottles! Obviously I give it a good wash afterwards, but that's my confession.

37, Canada

I lick plates.

50, UK

I was quite sexually active before I got married. When I got married I wanted to make sure that I tried everything at least once, so somehow I convinced my husband to let me give him a golden shower. He didn't want to make a mess so he said he would lay down in the bathtub. I squatted over him and I peed. it was not sexy at all. I'm pretty sure I looked like the Michelin tyre man from his angle. And he said my urine smelled strongly of coffee. So embarrassing. But I can say I did it, right?

26, Canada

My ex and I were staying at my sister's house. We got a bit frisky and I ended up wanking him off, but in true *There's Something About Mary* style, we couldn't find the come anywhere! Eventually we realized it had shot onto the velvet curtains, and I couldn't get it out! He rang his sister and told her we had got chicken soup on the curtains and what could we use to clean it off? Chicken soup!

The stain stayed there and I didn't tell my sister for years!

47, UK

Me and my husband went out to eat. It was right at the beginning of COVID, so we picked up take-out and went and had a date in the car. We parked in the parking lot of a church, and after we ate I had to poop. We lived a half hour away but I had to go bad, so I shat in the bag that our food came in while in the car and we left the bag of trash and faeces in the parking lot of the church. It wasn't solid shit either.

35, US

When I was in high school, I came home way past curfew one night. My mom had locked me out of the house and I had to use the restroom soooooo bad. Unfortunately, I had to go for a #2.

I found a plastic bag in the garage and napkins from the glove compartment of the car. I went in the bag, wiped with napkins, tied it all up and put it straight into the garbage bin. I have NEVER told anyone this story.

43, US

My husband and I were messing around – a "69" to be exact. In the middle of it, I got the urge to sneeze and ended up peeing on his face. We got a good laugh out of it but I've never seen him run to the shower so fast.

30, US

I was having sexual intercourse with my man of two and a half years, and going at it when SUDDENLY there was a gush. I had a terrible feeling it came from the back passage as I sometimes have a lactose problem with milk. I think it was that (ssshh), so anyway I cleaned up in the bathroom and then I went back in the bedroom and said, "Oh, I'm so sorry, babe. That's just old blood." He to this day thinks that.

39, UK

When I was 15 I had my first kiss in a back alley. My older sister had told me to hold my breath when I kissed him so I tried, but I couldn't hold my breath and all this snot came out of my nose and went in his mouth. I could hear laughter and I looked up and my sister and her friend were watching.

I was mortified. I have never spoken about it since and I'm 50 now.

50, UK

At Creamfields festival an acquaintance accused me of stealing her cigarettes. I swore blind it wasn't me, and it wasn't, but she kicked off and made me look like a dick, so when she went to the stages I had a shit in the bottom of her sleeping bag! it was fuelled by lots of alcohol so wasn't even a solid one either! When she climbed in that night with her bare feet the revenge was priceless!

28, UK

My husband is in the military so when he comes home from a deployment we are very very horny (as you can imagine –

deployments last months!). One afternoon, when he surprised us with an early return, we snuck upstairs while our two children aged two and six played in their room. After a sneaky quickie we got dressed as our eldest walked into the room. Phew, that was close, we thought. Until our son asked why there was "snot" on the floor. Yep, I had leaked some come in my rush to get dressed!

Quickest thinking ever was needed, and then it hit me. "Mummy has hay fever and has sneezed." He totally bought it.

33, UK

I once got my period in the middle of my exam. I had a habit of not wearing underwear as it gives me rashes, and I didn't keep track of my period because it is never late and I wasn't sexually active.

I considered my options when I felt my vagina leaking, but decided . . . fuck it, we will figure this out later. I sat in a way which keeps the blood from spilling out of the vag. It helped a bit. I did the exam, got up, went to the washroom, washed the loose trousers I was wearing and waited in the washroom for an hour to let it dry.

27, India

When I was in labour with my second, my waters still hadn't broken and I was already 8cm dilated. I was walking around doing my breathing exercises, etc, when I suddenly felt a gush of liquid come out. I was delighted, thinking it was my waters, only to discover it was actually wee. I peed myself all over the hospital floor with people watching. It was as magical as they say childbirth is in the movies. So magical . . .

32, Israel

A while back I had the Mirena coil. I was well into a very good "session" when blood starts to come out. I have a sensitive cervix so thought this was pretty normal and carried on. After, I get off to go and clean up, but it just didn't seem like it was me bleeding. I walked back into the bedroom to see my partner as white as a ghost and holding his rather floppy todger, at this point pouring out with blood. The coil had slit him from the top to the bottom of the helmet. He still has a scar.

27, UK

I had an appointment with my gyne yesterday. She asked me to cough when she was doing an internal exam. I coughed, she jumped and when I stood up to get dressed, I noticed her scrub pants were quite wet. Neither of us said anything.

I'm assuming it's part of the job, but a first for me and a reminder to empty the bladder before future appointments.

51, Canada

I tried a butt plug one time. It didn't have a stopper on the end and my butt swallowed it. I panicked, but swiftly remembered "I push out bigger shits than this", so covered the loo in toilet roll and pooped the thing out.

Now I always use one with a stopper.

27, UK

When I gave birth to my eldest, my labour went crazy stupid fast. Not that I was upset about that, but . . . ow. I had approached my due date with the idea that I'd be in labour for hours and hours, when in reality I was only in the hospital for two hours before she arrived. However, I had been awake for 48 hours straight before that, freaking out about when she was going to come and if she was going to arrive before her dad had to go back out of state for work (she made it with two days to spare). So while all laid out in the hospital bed, spread eagled, my husband and midwife say I completely passed out while pushing. I came to and finished what I had to do, but I also tore pretty well.

Afterwards, I would take a few minutes after every shower with a mirror down at my cooter, figuring out why the hell it looked so weird and wondering if it would go back. No big deal UNTIL my mother-in-law walked in on me standing there with a mirror down south and me pulling and pushing on all my bits down there, trying to figure it out. I was completely mortified, and we have never talked about what she saw that day and it's been three years now.

— 23, US —

I am a special needs teacher and we have an amazing swimming programme. Seriously, our therapists kick ass.

So we have all the kids in the pool and this brown thing floats up next to me. I'm right in front of the lifeguard so I look and It's a fucking FLOATER TURD. I didn't know what to do so I grab the damn thing and keep it in my hand for the entire hour we had adaptive swim. Why would I do that?

Because if this happens they have to shut down the pool for TWO WEEKS. My co-worker kept looking at me like I was an idiot and I couldn't get her to understand why I couldn't help with the one-on-one kids. After we get out of the pool and into the locker room, I told her what happened and we were pissing our pants.

— 31, US —

I took my baby swimming while my older child had a swimming lesson. The baby and I got out before the lesson ended to get changed and I REALLY needed a pee. I didn't want to leave the baby alone in the changing cubicle, so I did a pee into one of his nappies and never told anyone!

40, UK

My eldest son suffered from severe constipation as a baby due to a milk allergy and was unable to poop by himself. The doctor prescribed him lots of laxatives and gave me tips on how I could help him go. One of these tips was using Vaseline to massage and stimulate "poop movement". One particular day I was trying this "poop movement" tip only to suddenly end up in the firing line! For such a tiny person he had such a MASSIVE EXPLOSION! I am not kidding, there was green poop EVERYWHERE! All over the walls, the bed, all over ME and, worst of all, a nice chunk of it IN MY MOUTH! The smell and taste lingered for ages.

24, UK

I was constipated and there had been several days of no pooping so my doctor decided that I needed to take an enema. Having never done this before, I took out the box to read the instructions and thought "No problem".

I lie on my side on the floor and I put in the enema and I wait, then I get on the toilet and the water just comes out. No poop, just brown water comes out. By this point my stomach hurts and I'm really uncomfortable and I decide I should do it again as there's two in the box. So I lay back down on my side and take out the second one and insert ALL the medicine inside. I'm lying on my side and, unlike the first one, this time it starts to work really quickly. I'm like, "Oh crap," (no pun intended) but this is really happening.

So I hop up on my just surgically operated leg, which was a bad idea! The excruciating pain makes me scream really loud and I shit everywhere just as my husband comes running into the bathroom. I tell him to stop because it's everywhere and I make it to the toilet but I am sitting in shit all over the toilet. Poop is all over the floor but my husband doesn't stop because he's concerned about his wife who just had surgery screaming in the bathroom, so he comes flying around the corner with no shoes on and starts to slide in all the you-know-what. With arms flailing, here I am stuck on the toilet having explosive diarrhoea and my husband is sliding around in it.

I start to laugh and he starts to cry, and I am . . . still pooping . . . I can't stop.

It was the funniest and yet most humiliating moment of our married life. We have not told a soul. He scrubbed the floors, we scrubbed ourselves and threw away all the towels and clothes. We promised to never speak of it again.

46, US

When I was doing my teacher training, we had a session once every few weeks at a small school. It had one dodgy toilet for 30 adults for a three-hour session, so you always tried to go to the loo before arriving at the school.

One day a few people had already gone to the loo and I just couldn't hold it any more so had to brave it, having been told it wasn't flushing very well. I had a massive poo and of course the toilet wouldn't flush at all. The banter started about my toilet habits while I was trying to flush the toilet for ten minutes to no avail. In the end I had to fish the poo out of the toilet with toilet paper and put it in the bin as it wasn't possible to cover it any other way.

27, UK

Imagine the scene. You're heavily pregnant, your baby and organs are pressing on your bowel on a daily basis and the need to poo at work increases on a daily basis.

One day I was sat in my office, starting to sweat a little as I knew it was coming. There was no chance of holding it in until I got home because my unborn child's limbs are slowly massaging my internal passages and basically pushing the poo out.

I speed waddle down the corridor to the two toilets available, knowing that one of the toilets blocks when you even pee in it. To my utter devastation, that's the only loo available. So in I pop in the nick of time as the magic is just about to happen and, as feared, upon flushing the water rises and rises almost as quickly as my panic!

The water just sits there under the toilet rim, completely clear with a solitary log floating on the top. The toilet paper has gone and got wedged – as always!

The sweat is pouring out of my bloated pregnant body as I panic, knowing I can't walk away. Luckily the toilet is also the cleaning cupboard. In a moment of panicked genius I grabbed a tiny bin liner for the wastepaper bins and scoop my poo out of the toilet. I then had to stand and listen and make sure no one was outside. Knowing the other loo had been vacated, I fling myself in there and drop my poo out of the bag and into the other toilet. But what to do with the bloody shit bag? After ramming it into the sanitary bin, I mopped my sweaty brow, washed my hands within an inch of their lives and then I had to go and tell the building manager the loo was blocked and claim to have no knowledge. After what I can only describe as an Oscar-winning performance (even though there was clearly guilt all over my face), I retreated to my office and died a little bit inside at the horror of it all.

37, UK

I went to the hospital a month or so ago for a cystoscopy – an exploration of the bladder via the urethra. The consultant was doing what they do and I looked up to find my lady parts on the big screen. That's not the worst part.

The recovery initially didn't seem too bad, just mild stinging. But then came the swelling – dear god, the swelling. I was too embarrassed to tell anyone that it wasn't pain I was experiencing but the constant sensation that I needed to "finish myself off".

I tried heat packs and cold compresses pressed against my bits but NOTHING worked. I Googled every day but this is not a side effect anyone has ever written about (funny, that). I was too scared to get myself off in case it made things worse rather than relieved the pressure. I spent two excruciatingly long weeks like this and I was convinced I'd never go back to normal. I'm happy to report everything is fine and in working order now though.

38, UK

I put my son on a time out in his room when he was two, and all went quiet. And we all know kids are up to no good when they are quiet . . .

Well, after a few minutes in his room, I checked on him. As soon as I opened the door, all I could smell was POOP. Looking around, I asked my son, "Did you poop?" He looked at me and points to his humidifier. HE SHAT IN HIS HUMIDIFIER!

At this point as a parent with a two-year-old and a newborn, I didn't know whether to laugh or cry. I chose to laugh! What else can you do? I truly believe he was trying to help and took it out of his diaper and put it in there. Thanks for helping, baby boy. I love you!

30, Canada

When I was 12 or so, I went to the doctor for an appointment. While there I had to leave a urine sample. I walked out of the bathroom, trying to be all ladylike, and ended up tripping over a bump in the carpet. I had not closed the lid all the way and end up spilling the whole urine sample all down the hallway! With the door to the lobby open and a cute boy in the waiting room.

37, US

When I was working in a gym, I had to be up at 4am each day. Sometimes I had to come off a late shift at 10pm, get home at 11.30pm, and be back out of the door by 5am. When this happened my clothes would get thrown in a heap, ready for me to dress in the dark the next morning. One day my fiancé was feeling frisky, so I stripped off, undies included, and had some fun. I shoved my clothes on the next morning and went about my business. I went shopping on my break and got a tap on the shoulder. "Er, excuse me," said the fittest guy ever. "These just fell out of your trouser leg." He was holding my undies from the day before!

39, UK

When I was younger I really fancied this guy who was on the outskirts of our friend group. One night I invited everyone back to my flat after a night out, hoping he would come too. He did and I was so excited – and very drunk. I managed to orchestrate him staying and everyone else leaving.

Hoorah, I had him to myself! Trying to be a mix of mysterious elegance and playful tease, I decided to do a headstand. I don't know why, I'd never done one before.

I was in a skirt and I asked him to catch my legs. As I drunkenly attempted my headstand, my legs very inelegantly fell agape. He politely gathered my wayward limbs and, in a very gentlemanly gesture, pushed my legs together again.

Unfortunately I'd obviously gathered some air during my acrobatic manoeuvre and, as he moved my legs together, the loudest muff guff, fanny fart, queef – whatever you care to call it – exited my body with such force that, I swear to god, his hair moved. I was devastated and we both froze exactly as we were. Him holding my legs with a look of disgust on his face and me in a headstand, blushing red, with my skirt around my middle and my knickers on show. Neither of us acknowledged the muff guff, which was hilarious as it had the volume of an elephant's trumpet. He gently lowered me down and gathered his things. I never saw him again.

52, UK

A few years ago I went to a party with a friend. About halfway through the night, when both of us were very merry, my friend took me into a different room at the back of the house where a friend was arranging lines of cocaine! To say I was surprised is an understatement.

My friend gave her friend some money then proceeded to do a line. I was standing there embarrassed and uncomfortable when she said, "Your turn." I said no, as I'd never done any kind of drugs, but her friends and the one selling the stuff started to put on the pressure. In the end I went forward to take a line. I was given a straw and told how to do it. I started to snort it, but wasn't expecting it to tickle my nose, to the extent that I did a huge sneeze right in front of the table, in front of everyone and the other lines of laid out coke. You can guess what happened when I sneezed – the coke went everywhere! The look on the dealer's face and my friend's face was priceless. The dealer had a beard which was pure black, but after my epic sneeze it was now a salt and pepper shade. The room had gone from everyone cheering me on to complete and utter silence; you could have heard a pin drop!

I was horrified and started apologizing, trying to explain I'd never done it before and that it had tickled my nose. My friend just chucked some more money at him, grabbed my hand and pulled me out of the room and then the house. That was the one and only time I tried hard drugs.

— 52, UK—

Since having three kids, two husbands and a hysterectomy, I have to wear bladder control pads.

— 47, Australia—

Good Luck!

There you have it – confessions from around the world. It was hard to narrow them down because every secret sent in meant something to the person who wrote and I would have liked to share them all.

Personally, whenever I've ever had a secret, I've always felt better once it was out in the open. As awful as it may have been, or as scared as I was of what people would think of me, the worries never measured up to the reality. It was never as bad as I thought it would be, and I hope something in this book makes you see that. Perhaps you are holding on to a secret and it's weighing you down, or perhaps you've read someone else's confession that reminds you of your own . . . My hope is that it's helped you see that it's not as bad as you think.

We hide many aspects of ourselves, sometimes even from those most close to us, and in the age of social media this has become even more true. Why is it easier to be vulnerable online with an audience of strangers, often at the expense of being truly vulnerable in real life with our loved ones? Who we truly are is all we can ever really be, yet we spend our whole lives trying to fit in or be more like other people. Being truthful and honest sets us free and I sincerely hope this is one of the things people take away from this book.

And on a less serious note, I hope you laughed.

I often get asked how I am able to laugh about the most difficult things but, truth be told, I rarely laugh in the moment, only later … Sometimes much, much later.

That day I stabbed the cupcakes after my kids drove me crazy, I met up with a friend for a walk (so that I wouldn't end up stabbing the roast chicken too). I stormed up to her and just started venting, telling her the entire story of how I ended up hacking at my kid's cupcakes in our kitchen bin with a wooden spoon while screaming 'No one is getting the cupcakes!' Here's another confession for you – a few years ago I would not have told her. Or anyone. I would have just felt lots of guilt and shame and hidden it from my friends. If I'd ever mentioned it, I would have probably made it sound not as bad as it actually was. I'd have downplayed it, laughed off the scene and the feelings that caused it.

But years of reading confessions has taught me better and I know now that human emotions are universal, that we all have rage, jealousy and weird things we do (like sitting in the shower), and that the sooner I got it out, the sooner I'd feel better about it.

As I stood there in the middle of the street telling her about my afternoon, we were both able to laugh together and she admitted to a similar experience.

I hope you are relieved to read the proof that everyone has secrets, and that some of them are worse than yours …

Acknowledgements

This one is easy.

Every single person who has ever sent in a confession for Pyjama Party & Confessions, for any of my live shows and, of course, for this book deserves to be acknowledged and thanked. It doesn't matter if their confession was sent in because they hoped they might win a prize (most nights there was no prize at all apart from the community's support and respect); the fact that they were willing to be vulnerable, to put themselves out there and take part in what I think has become a bit of a social experiment (can we actually listen to people's deepest secrets without judging them?) is so brave and so inspiring and I will forever be grateful for that trust. Whether your confession was featured or not does not matter, the fact you took the time to send it in means so much.

I would also like to thank my publishers at Watkins Media who were on board with the idea of a confessions book from Day One. I am grateful for their hard work, professionalism and support, but most of all for their enthusiasm and for getting it! My goal was not to just share sensational stories, but also to make people feel better about themselves knowing they're not alone (while giving them a good belly laugh at the same time).

And finally, thank you to my family. To my husband, Mike, and our three daughters, whom I love more than life itself. I could not have done it without you.

About the Author

Tova Leigh is a writer, performer and humourist who creates regular content for her global community of over 1.6m people worldwide. Born in Israel, where she practised as a lawyer, Tova moved to the UK to study drama, and in 2015 started her hugely successful blog "My Thoughts About Stuff", which propelled her to internet stardom with her impassioned, hilarious and honest takes on parenthood, marriage, body confidence and sex. She since counts an Amazon Prime documentary film *Mom Life Crisis*, her bestselling debut book *F*cked at 40*, a weekly podcast "Till Death Do Us Pod" and countless live shows as further strings to her impressive bow, as she continues to use her platform to support, empower and celebrate women.

She resides in London with her husband and their three girls. *You Did WHAT?* is her second book, based on her hugely successful Facebook live show – "Pyjama Party and Confessions".

Find out more at: www.tovaleigh.com

WATKINS
Sharing Wisdom Since 1893

The story of Watkins began in 1893, when scholar of esotericism John Watkins founded our bookshop, inspired by the lament of his friend and teacher Madame Blavatsky that there was nowhere in London to buy books on mysticism, occultism or metaphysics. That moment marked the birth of Watkins, soon to become the publisher of many of the leading lights of spiritual literature, including Carl Jung, Rudolf Steiner, Alice Bailey and Chögyam Trungpa.

Today, the passion at Watkins Publishing for vigorous questioning is still resolute. Our stimulating and groundbreaking list ranges from ancient traditions and complementary medicine to the latest ideas about personal development, holistic wellbeing and consciousness exploration. We remain at the cutting edge, committed to publishing books that change lives.

DISCOVER MORE AT:
www.watkinspublishing.com

Read our blog

Watch and listen to
our authors in action

Sign up to
our mailing list

We celebrate conscious, passionate, wise and happy living.
Be part of that community by visiting

 /watkinspublishing   @watkinswisdom

 /watkinsbooks   @watkinswisdom